EMOTIONAL MASTERY for RELATIONSHIPS

7 Communication Strategies for a Drama-Free Life

ARDA OZDEMIR

Author, *The Art of Becoming Unstuck*

RISE 2 REALIZE

Copyright © 2024 Arda Ozdemir

All rights reserved.

No part of this book may be reproduced, or stored in a retrieval system, or transmitted in any form or by any means, electronic, mechanical, photocopying, recording, or otherwise, without express written permission of the publisher.

Emotional Mastery for Relationships is for informational and educational purposes only. The information contained in this guidebook is based on the author's own experience and not intended to diagnose, prescribe, treat, or cure any disease or mental condition, or to replace the services of a licensed therapist, mental health care provider, or physician.

Published by Rise 2 Realize LLC, Los Altos, CA www.rise2realize.com

Developmental and Line Editing: Dakota Nyght www.dakotanyght.com
Copyediting: Lore Alexander www.scribeandsunshine.com
Proofreading: Lia Ottaviano on Reedsy.com
Content Advisor: Elizabeth Ouellette www.bestlifeevercoach.com

Cover Design: Kathryn Campbell www.inkbooksdesign.com
Image credits: Cover Photo © iStockphoto/StellaLevi
Author photo © Tati Scutelnic www.tatiratita.com

ISBN (paperback): 978-0-9898104-3-2
ISBN (ebook): 978-0-9898104-4-9

First edition

Printed in the United States of America

RISE 2 REALIZE

CONTENTS

Introduction	The Birth of a Life-Changing Method	1
Chapter One	Experiencing a Different Life	13
Chapter Two	Awakening to the Present Moment	23
Chapter Three	Observing the Unseen	55
Chapter Four	Going Beyond the Mind	91
Chapter Five	Moving from Chaos to Calm	125
Chapter Six	From Learning to Living	155
Conclusion	Rise Above Drama	171
Appendix One		175
Appendix Two		179
About the Author		182

INTRODUCTION

The Birth of a Life-Changing Method

It was the summer of 1985. I was in Essen, Germany, doing a summer internship to practice my German. One day, I went for a walk in a public park nearby. In front of me, I noticed an older woman and a man, probably in their late seventies, walking hand in hand. What made them so special was how sweet and cute their affection for each other was.

I'd rarely seen an older couple show such loving interaction in public. Can you imagine PDA with your spouse in your seventies? Well, I was eighteen years old back then, too young to think about my older years, yet the sight of this lovely German couple made quite an impression on me. I immediately thought, *my parents should hold hands like that and display their love when they walk side by side.*

Upon my return home to Istanbul, I immediately asked my parents if they could hold each other's hand when walking together. Even though my invitation was somewhat peculiar and uncomfortable for them, to be fair, they tried it a few times. But it wasn't in them. It was too obvious that they didn't feel anything. I could tell they were simply not connected. I knew they loved each other. But I guess, sadly, they were not in love anymore. After those few times, I never saw them comply with my wish again.

This realization wasn't new. Throughout my childhood, I'd seen them argue almost daily. They'd sit at the dinner table without saying a word. As time passed, they became increasingly irritable and impatient with each other over small things. You can tell I already knew my parents' unhappiness. But, like any child, I wanted to see them happy.

I tried my best. I was a sensitive child. I later realized that it was not just my parents who were discontent in their relationships. Unhappiness was everywhere. It was like an epidemic. Wherever I looked, I could feel people's unhappiness, whether they were my parents' friends, my friends' parents, or whoever else. It didn't matter. People were unhappy. This low feeling was palpable everywhere in society. It affected me deeply. I developed a strong desire to make others happy. As a result, I spent my entire adolescence as a people pleaser.

HOW MY PAST BECAME MY FUTURE

After a few decades of people-pleasing, I realized that I couldn't accomplish my goal of making others happy on a one-on-one basis. I needed something methodical to help more people and relationships see better days. This quest later turned into a mission, where I started reading many books to figure out how relationships really work, what exactly makes everyone so unhappy, and how they can eventually find the path to happiness.

The books were not enough though. I needed more tangible evidence to develop a powerful method that would fundamentally change people's lives. The opportunity to fulfill this desire came when I left the corporate world in February 2011 to pursue my calling as a life coach. Since then, more than six thousand couples and individuals have reached out to me for advice. Like my parents, most of them had lost their connection and grown apart in their romantic relationships. Others had trouble communicating and connecting with their kids. A few of them experienced fallouts with their bosses, colleagues, and friends, not to mention in-laws and neighbors.

I am grateful to have worked with such a variety of clients from all walks of life. As I conducted one session after another, I started getting deeper insights and a fuller understanding of human conditioning and what makes people unhappy in their romantic, personal, and professional interactions with others.

As a result of these profound findings, my mission to discover the root cause of why so many relationships fail started to bear fruit. When I put all my notes and observations together, everything boiled down to one simple yet complicated phenomenon:

Drama destroys relationships!

After all, everyone has a sense of what happiness looks like, but being happy is another story altogether. For this reason, it's not for lack of trying but for lack of knowledge in how to eliminate drama from life. Unresolved conflicts plague all relationships, creating enormous distance between people. Each poorly managed dramatic event disrupts lives and creates monsters and enemies among lovers, pulling them into endless arguments, constant bickering, and silent treatments.

Whether such conflicts stem from a lack of communication or compatibility among couples or simply result from differences in values, expectations, spending habits, or parenting styles, we all struggle to deal with them. We simply don't have the tools to resolve such drama that destroys connections between people.

Going back to my parents' relationship, I knew, at least from the pictures I saw of them courting each other, that it was a love marriage. I could see how happy they were. Their chemistry was vibrant, magnetic, and visible to everyone. They were always the first couple on the dance floor to open the dance on Friday and Saturday nights when a live band played at their social club in a small town called Karabük, where I was born.

Their relationship was supposed to be a fairy tale, but within a few years, it turned into a drama-filled battlefield. I was dying to know what had happened. How did that love disappear? What went wrong? What causes the downfall of a happy marriage? How does drama creep in and destroy people's lives?

THE NIGHT I RUINED EVERYTHING

Maybe a specific anecdote from my marriage that I experienced fifteen years ago could shed some light on these questions and give us clues on where to deepen our investigation of why relationships struggle.

Here I was, on a Friday night, going on a dinner date with my wife. We'd been eagerly looking forward to this romantic night. The past few months had been tough on us, and we had many stressful moments. So we decided it would be great to try a new restaurant everyone had been raving about and spend quality time together.

I took care of the reservation and specifically asked the restaurant to set us up at a nice, private table. I wanted to spend some intimate time with the love of my life. The night started off very well. We were driving toward San Francisco, and our timing was perfect. We could see the sunset on the horizon. While watching the last remnants of the bright orange sun, we had a fun, joyful, and interactive conversation. We both felt deeply connected to each other.

While everything was seemingly going well, with lots of laughter and intimacy, all of a sudden, my wife interrupted our conversation with worry in her voice. She almost screamed, "Why are you driving so close to the car in front of us?"

Her remark caught me off guard. The interruption immediately derailed my excitement about the romantic night ahead. To my surprise, I started to experience anger as a hot, boiling flush slowly rising toward my head. On the steering wheel, my hands clenched up. I was in shock. I couldn't think or talk, and I felt completely paralyzed about what to do.

At that moment, I tried very hard not to lose it. I didn't want to ruin the night. Yet I couldn't help it. I raised my voice in frustration and said, "Why are you controlling me? I'm not tailgating." Then I sarcastically added, "If you think you're a better driver, why don't you take over?"

She immediately responded, "Why are you being so snappy and rude? Are you getting defensive again? I just told you to slow down!"

Of course, her comment made me angrier, and I raised my voice even more. "Well, if you didn't try to control me, we would be doing just fine. Didn't you see? There was enough space, and I was driving carefully. Why do you have to get into my business and ruin my mood? You always do that!"

Then she started yelling at me. "Whaaat?! Are you blaming me now? Why is it always my fault that you lose your cool and take my simple comments so personally?"

After that, we got into one of those endless "he said, she said" arguments that you may be familiar with from your own relationships.

Of course, the exchange ruined both our moods. I stayed quiet and gave my wife the silent treatment for almost the entire dinner. She did the same to me. Finally, when more than an hour and a half had passed, I cooled off and broke the silence. As dessert was served, I put on my pouty face and said, "Look, I'm sorry for ruining our night! I don't know why I lose my cool, but it always happens. I wish we could find a better way to deal with these situations."

My wife, still upset, replied, "But, Arda, you always get angry and blame me whenever I say something. Why are you so sensitive? We're not enemies."

I started to feel frustrated again and tried one more time to make my point. "But, honey, you always use a condescending tone toward me, as if I'm doing something wrong. Of course I'm going to take it personally. What should I do? Should I just sit there and do nothing when you're putting me down? I can't seem to do anything right in your eyes."

My wife interrupted my vent and calmly said, "It's not my tone but how you perceive it, Arda. I never mean to put you down. I was merely stating how close we had gotten to the car in front of us, and it worried me. I had to say something because I was getting anxious. What has that got to do with you?"

I got quiet and started reflecting on what my wife was saying. I didn't admit it right there and then, but she was right. I was calmer because so much time had passed since our argument. I realized that I'd made a big deal out of nothing. But at the time, I didn't know why I was offended. As a matter of fact, I felt exactly that every time she made a comment about me or what I was doing.

After a few minutes of silence, I gathered my courage and admitted my guilt with a soft and defeated tone, "I'm sorry again. I don't know why I react the way I do, but your comments certainly didn't warrant my reaction. I'll think about what you just said. And I'll try not to react and take your words personally next time. Are you okay?"

She smiled back and nodded with silent agreement, although I could tell she was still feeling a little upset and was probably doubtful that anything would change until our following argument. But with these sour sentiments, we clinked our dessert spoons together in a toast to turn an unhappy moment into a smile.

MY LACK OF AWARENESS

On the surface, it's not rocket science to see what went wrong here. Clearly, my emotional reaction created the drama and ruined the night for both of us. My wife was merely commenting to share her feelings of anxiety with me and wanted me to slow down so that she felt safe. Instead of responding to her needs, I took her suggestion personally and reacted emotionally to her—thus derailing us from a memorable date night!

However, at a deeper level, I didn't know why I perceived her suggestions or comments as condescending. I had no clue why I got offended. I didn't understand why I was so upset and angry when all she was doing was to point out what worried her. It was highly concerning and puzzling when I reflected on how quickly I reacted to her. I simply had no control over my words, actions, or emotions. I was just blurting them out. I'd set up a beautiful date night, and we were both in such great moods; why did I have to instantly blame my wife for her comments?

After switching my career from the high rankings of the corporate world to the intimate sessions of life coaching, I realized years later that I simply didn't have the self-awareness, nor the understanding required to know where my emotions came from. I didn't have the skills to regulate my emotional reactions. I blurted out whatever came up. My automatic reaction was the cause of drama. My response kicked off those unstoppable back-and-forth arguments, which caused a downward spiral and ruined our night.

The sad thing is that it was not the first time I took a comment personally. I'd done this so many times, emotionally reacting to someone so intensely that it ruined a night, a connection, or a relationship. Yes, I alienated family members, friends, colleagues, and others. Even though the drama I created came from a lack of self-awareness, I didn't see myself as part of the problem for many years.

In those years, I thought others were at fault. They were the ones to blame. They needed to change their behaviors. I didn't get angry; they made me angry. Their actions caused me frustration. Why would I react to them otherwise? Yes, it was definitely more straightforward—and automatic self-defense—to blame their actions for my outbursts. Looking back, I'd say I was pretty hypocritical and unwilling to take responsibility for my emotional reactions.

With that arrogance and ignorance in those years, I missed the train left and right. I ruined many special moments. I simply couldn't enjoy meaningful experiences and deep connections with loved ones. Again, it was not until I started practicing life coaching and investigating this phenomenon of why we take things so personally that I realized that the path to happiness began with me.

As I deepened my quest to investigate the root cause of unhappiness in relationships, I got profound insights from reading psychological, philosophical, and spiritual texts. From these materials and the workshops and courses I attended about similar subjects, I realized that I had to first learn about myself, namely, who I was and why I emotionally reacted to people.

This realization helped me develop a step-by-step method I could apply to myself to thoroughly understand the source of my intense emotional reactions. After seeing some transformative results in how I managed my emotions, I decided to share the same method with my clients to see if they could achieve similar results in regulating their own emotional reactions. One session after another, the results started to come in. Those who applied the techniques experienced less intense, in some cases, moderate or light emotional reactions, which led to clearer communications, better relationships, and deeper connections with others.

THE BIRTH OF A LIFE-CHANGING METHOD

After all, I had to put in personal work and test the techniques through my own life experiences to have the results and the confidence to share the Method with my clients. My self-discovery journey began in this context. I had to dig deep to figure out who I was and what was going on inside me during my emotional reactivity. My curiosity slowly turned into a quest. As I mentioned, I read many books and attended workshops, seminars, and classes to learn tools and techniques, making me more aware of myself.

Once I gained deeper insights into my psyche and conditioning, I decided to test whether what I was learning and experiencing could be translated and formed into a powerful, effective, and practical method that could help me and others.

From the beginning of my journey, when I left the corporate world to pursue my calling of helping others find happiness, my goal had always been to create a universal method practical enough that anybody could use it in their daily interactions (so that I could stop being a people pleaser). Yes, I wanted to create something so special that whoever picked up the method could learn to regulate their emotional reactions, eliminate drama from their relationships, and prevent themselves from spiraling into unhappiness.

What you are about to read is the result of that journey and the Method that emerged from my research, investigation, and analysis of human conditioning. Experiencing this Method in my own life and seeing it yield profound results in my clients' lives gave me the assurance and confidence to understand what creates drama in relationships and ruins connections.

Every session, I eagerly took copious notes to explore more about life and about who we are as individuals. These one-on-one interactions with my clients provided me with invaluable information about why we do things the way we do. They provided huge opportunities to tweak, test, experiment, examine, and define my tools and techniques. As I created the step-by-step Method, I implemented it in my sessions to better understand how to guide someone toward emotional mastery.

Five distinct steps emerged when I carefully combined the most effective tools and techniques. They came together so well that they created a harmonious flow anyone could follow to manage their emotions and turn their reactions into mindful communications.

How do you do that?

Imagine you're in one of those heated arguments with your spouse. What if you managed to pause right in the middle of your emotional reactions? Then, what if you observed the thoughts and feelings that made you take that situation personally? After that, what if you welcomed any arising emotions and related physical sensations in the body? And finally, what if you knew how to discharge this emotional intensity to the earth through a process called earthing? If you followed these steps, would you be better positioned to mindfully respond to your spouse instead of getting lost in your emotional reactions and feeling stuck in those destructive drama cycles?

When I put together the initials of each step as described above—*pause, observe, welcome, earth, and respond*—they magically spelled *power*. It was quite interesting to name the Method "Power" because our emotional reactions often come from a state of powerlessness. In a sense, this Method is designed to give you back the power that you usually lose to others out of your defensiveness. You will not use this newly acquired skill to overpower others but to create a strong presence to stay calm and grounded in the midst of drama.

As soon as these steps came together, I started sharing them with my clients during our sessions. They have learned and used them over the years to effectively regulate their emotional reactions and create drama-free relationships. Their success became the proof of this life-changing step-by-step protocol.

At the same time, the 5-Step Power Method is more than just a set of techniques. It's a skill you can use to transform your life and get unstuck from your negative drama cycles. As a side benefit, you gain mental clarity on difficult life decisions when you become less reactive. You'll inevitably make better choices. Whether you're dealing with relationship drama, work stress, or personal struggles, this practical Method helps you turn your life around and empowers you to live as your best version.

You don't need to believe in this Method for it to work. You just need to test it and experiment with it. Then, simply observe the results and experience what happens after you apply it. After that, you can conclude whether it's for you or not.

Let the positive shift in your emotional reactions and what you experience afterward be the evidence. Let every success inspired by this step-by-step protocol provide you with the inner knowing that you can indeed regulate your automatic, unconscious emotional reactions. No matter how severe the conflict is, you gain the confidence and inner strength to come up with thoughtful, conscious responses and prevent any dire situation from escalating into drama.

Your commitment and consistency with the tools and techniques described in this book will help you go far and deep on your journey. Then, the only remaining question is whether you feel ready to discover how this life-changing Method can work for you and unlock a new level of emotional intelligence that will positively impact every area of your life. The journey to greater self-awareness and drama-free relationships is about to begin. Knowing what's ahead, I'm truly excited for you to experience the profound changes that await on your path to happiness.

CHAPTER ONE

EXPERIENCING A DIFFERENT LIFE

The Wonders of Emotional Mastery

Imagine finding yourself in a similar heated argument with a loved one, where emotions are running high, and suddenly, words are flying out of your mouth faster than you can think. We've all been there and experienced such painful moments that later fill us with regret and resentment. We've all wished things had gone differently so that we'd enjoy deeper and more meaningful connections with the people we love.

What if you could hit the pause button right there? What if you could magically step back, gather your thoughts, and transform those immediate, unconscious emotional reactions into something more thoughtful and mindful? This might sound like an unattainable dream, but it's entirely possible.

Many people, just like you, have discovered an approach that helps them do just that—turn their automatic reactions into conscious responses and experience the miracles of emotional mastery. This approach presents a personal journey of great magnitude that can change how you interact with the world around you.

In this chapter, I'm excited to share the details of this powerful emotional regulation method and the carefully designed Communication Strategies that accompany it. Together, we'll explore how to harness your emotions, leading to calmer interactions, deeper connections, and happier relationships.

Let's revisit my earlier personal anecdote and explore what would have happened if I had used the 5-Step Power Method and its 7 Communication Strategies, regulated my emotions, and reacted to my wife differently, maybe in a calmer, more grounded way.

Let's reroll the tape—this time with more awareness!

My wife and I are in the car, driving to dinner, when she suddenly comments, "Can you slow down? You're driving too fast and getting too close to the car in front of us."

I immediately feel my anger and frustration rising. But instead of reacting right away, I pause to notice what is coming up as an emotion.

Then I observe the thoughts going through my head as I hear her comments:

"My wife is closely watching how I'm driving. She's judging me that I'm a bad, careless driver!"

"My wife is constantly controlling me and telling me what to do. Enough is enough. She can't control me."

"My wife is always in my business. I can't be happy and cheerful. She always needs to criticize me and put me down."

While observing all that activity in my mind, I suddenly notice the tightness in my stomach. As I acknowledge these physical sensations, probably resulting from my anger, I inhale into my stomach and exhale all that tightness out of my body.

When I exhale, I imagine letting all that go out of my feet into the earth. I immediately feel grounded and centered and find myself in a better position with a stronger sense of presence to respond to her comments.

From that vantage point, I can now consciously choose to respond to my wife with a calmer tone. "Oh, I didn't realize we were getting too close. Let me back up a little bit. How does this distance feel for you?"

As you can imagine, it's a much better interaction, and of course, she responds with a happy smile. She okays the distance with a sigh of relief. Her anxiety subsides. We continue our conversation, and she eagerly engages with her thoughts and perspective.

This outcome is evidence of the miracles an emotional regulation method can bring to your relationships. You can achieve such emotional mastery by learning and practicing the 5-Step Power Method and experience a drama-free life as you regulate your emotional reactions.

What did I do in the above situation?

> First step: I *paused* to notice my emotional reactions to the trigger event.
>
> Second step: I *observed* my thoughts about the person or the situation.
>
> Third step: I *welcomed* the physical sensations resulting from my emotional reactions.
>
> Fourth step: I *earthed* the emotional charge I felt in my body as a sensation.
>
> Fifth step: I *responded* with more conscious statements to eliminate drama.

When applied in a seamless, harmonious flow, these steps will lead to emotional mastery. The word *power* only means "power over your own actions"—not power over others. When you consistently follow these steps to deal with emotional triggers, within a couple of months, you create a mental space where you consciously choose your responses to people instead of unconsciously reacting to them.

A famous quote usually attributed to Viktor Frankl, the author of

Man's Search for Meaning, describes this mental space extraordinarily well: "Between stimulus and response lies a space. In that space lies our freedom and power to choose a response. In our response lies our growth and our happiness."

Your life will never be the same again when you feel that space. From that moment on, you feel empowered to embrace every challenging situation confidently and trust that you can overcome any drama you face today. The rewards awaiting you are priceless. You are about to acquire a skill that will completely change your relationships. It will change everything and everyone around you.

It's not going to be an easy ride. How could it be? Mastering your emotions means going against your instinctive, unconscious fight-or-flight defense mechanisms, your automatic physiological reaction to a stressful event that prepares the body to fight or flee. Your subconscious mind will resist you until the cows come home. However, your desire and commitment to change your emotional reactions and eliminate drama from your relationships will eventually overcome every hurdle, whether internal or external.

THE BEGINNER'S MINDSET

You may already feel overwhelmed by the number of steps you need to follow. You probably think, like all my clients do in the beginning, that it is impossible to put this five-step protocol into practice in the heat of the moment. Yes, it is difficult to remember all of this when you're also emotionally reacting to an intense trigger.

However, isn't learning a new technique always an overwhelming experience? Like any new skill you learn, especially a profound life skill like this, the Power Method requires your commitment to repetition and an unyielding discipline for consistency until it becomes second nature.

You don't try to play a competitive game of tennis after only one or two lessons, do you? Even if you did, you wouldn't have a sense of where to place your feet, when to open your racket, how to shift your weight, how to hit the ball so it goes where you want it to go, how to follow through after your shot, and so on.

You need to practice all these little steps individually and then combine them in your practice sessions until you master them. Only then do you come out and play the game at your best, putting together all you learned until it becomes part of you and your life.

Similarly, you learn the 5-Step Power Method in incremental stages, mastering each before moving on to the next. Each step has specific techniques and accompanying strategies designed for your success in turning your emotional reactions into conscious responses during challenging interactions with others.

LEARNING HOW TO RESPOND

The 5-Step Power Method serves as an emotional regulation technique and prepares you to get out of your comfort zone and set healthy boundaries with proven, well-thought-out Communication Strategies.

You probably know from experience that communication is the cornerstone of any successful relationship. Whether with a partner, friend, family member, or colleague, the words you choose and how you express yourself can create bridges or build walls.

The specifically designed Communication Strategies that you're about to learn will transform your interactions into more meaningful and fulfilling exchanges. After regulating your emotional reactions, these strategies become essential response techniques to triggers that will help you raise your awareness and feel empowered to deal with difficult people and challenging situations. The shift in your communication will catalyze the drama-free relationships you've been looking for.

By the way, these strategies aren't just about saying the right thing; they're about listening actively and responding with empathy and understanding. By mastering these techniques along with your emotions, you'll find yourself expressing your thoughts and feelings more clearly and becoming more attuned to the emotional needs of those around you. Imagine the impact of having conversations that leave everyone feeling heard and valued.

Here are the 7 Communication Strategies you can use as the fifth step, respond, in the 5-Step Power Method. Every time you use these techniques effectively, you'll prevent arguments from escalating and have the chance to break free from the destructive drama cycles that plague your relationships.

> First strategy: Doing the Opposite
>
> Second strategy: Using I-Feel Statements
>
> Third strategy: Asking Open-Ended Curious Questions
>
> Fourth strategy: Holding Space with Attentive Listening
>
> Fifth strategy: Leveling with an Aikido Move
>
> Sixth strategy: Using I-Need Statements
>
> Seventh strategy: Asking Collaborative We Questions

Each strategy requires a certain level of awareness and understanding of your thought patterns and feelings. For example, you can't jump to the fifth strategy right off the bat and level a trigger event with an Aikido Move without fully digesting the energy and meaning of the previous four strategies. Therefore, keep in mind that the more advanced the Communication Strategy is, the more self-awareness you need to have.

Don't worry, though. These strategies, along with the steps of the Power Method, are all laid out like breadcrumbs throughout the book. By following the path and its guidance, you will easily progress with the 5-Step Power Method and learn the intricacies of each step and strategy.

WALKING THE PATH TO HAPPINESS TOGETHER

I hope you sense that you are about to embark on a significant personal transformation journey in pursuit of drama-free relationships, which will eventually lead you to more happy moments that last for longer periods of time. To get the best results, I recommend allocating one whole week to each Power Step. Practice them consistently and slowly integrate them into your daily life. Every chapter describes the theory behind these steps and provides the necessary tools and techniques to successfully execute them, along with the accompanying Communication Strategies.

Please note that all these strategies follow a specific sequence of consciousness. Each of them represents a certain level of awareness. Therefore, jumping from one to the other without understanding what is required for each step and strategy will yield unsatisfying results. I highly encourage you to vigorously work with one strategy for a while and try it at every opportunity before moving to the next one. Once you master each strategy individually, you can combine them during your response to a trigger event.

After completing all the steps, you may want to go back to the first one and start all over, but with higher self-awareness and deeper understanding from the experience of your previous round. In fact, you may want to circle back multiple times until the Power Method and its Communication Strategies become natural to you. After all, it's a skill you'll use for the rest of your life.

Remember, mastery comes from your failed attempts, not quick, shortcut successes. When you diligently practice every day, every week, every month, you'll naturally achieve the drama-free, happy, and—may I say—miraculous results you have been waiting for your entire life.

Along with completing the weekly assignments—yes, there will be some homework—I highly recommend allocating five to ten minutes for a review at the end of each day. This self-reflection time is essential for expanding your awareness and understanding of your emotional reactions. To help you with this practice, please download a PDF version of the Daily Review template at www.rise2realize.com/daily-review.

Keep in mind that failure is part of the journey. Learning from your mistakes and reflecting on the negative results of your strategies deepen your self-awareness even more. And through introspection and making constant adjustments to your Communication Strategies, sooner or later, you start to observe positive shifts in your life.

For example, you'll start to experience stronger emotional bonds and more empathetic connections. You'll sense a more harmonious flow in your interactions through reduced misunderstanding and miscommunication. When you become more open to expressing your feelings, listening to others' perspectives, and collaborating for mutually beneficial solutions, you and your partner will have a better ability to solve the lingering problems, increasing the quality of your relationship.

You're about to embark on a life-changing journey. I'd like to be there with you on every step of the path. To accomplish that goal, I have used a Q&A format where I respond to questions and thoughts presented as though we're walking side by side. I want to create a conversation between you and me instead of writing a textbook where I teach you about the theory of emotional mastery.

If you have any additional questions that arise from your experience with the Power Method and its Communication Strategies, please feel free to join me at one of our free in-person or online events we offer at Rise 2 Realize Institute, www.R2R.org/events.

I am wishing you all the best! Now, let's get on with our journey and take the first Power Step, pause, to slow down our automatic emotional reactions!

CHAPTER TWO

AWAKENING TO THE PRESENT MOMENT

The Power of the Pause

Your heart is racing, your palms are sweaty, and words are tumbling out of your mouth before you can even register the damage or hurt you're imposing on the other person or your relationship.

In another moment, you're staring at the screen of your computer or phone, and your finger is hovering over the 'send' button of an email or a text that you know you shouldn't send but somehow can't stop yourself.

Minutes, if not hours, later, you realize what you did. The negative self-talk rushes into your head. You can't shake off the self-deprecating thoughts. You keep wishing, "If only I'd paused for a moment...". But, deep down, you'll show another similar impulse pretty soon and find yourself yet again in embarrassing situations.

When is this going to end?

When you achieve emotional mastery, you'll experience fewer irreversible embarrassments. If you'd like to attain such levels of mastery, the first technique you want to learn is how to pause. That's why, in this chapter, we'll explore the transformative potential of Pause as the first Power Step. We'll delve into why our brains often bypass this crucial step and, more importantly, how we can train ourselves to harness its remarkable abilities.

You may not know this, but the ability to pause, collect your thoughts, and transform the automatic, knee-jerk reactions into mindful responses and meaningful conversations is literally at your fingertips. You may not believe in yourself to have the capacity to do it. But, over time, you'll discover how simple yet profound tools could change how you communicate, make decisions, and navigate life's most challenging moments.

Why do I have these knee-jerk reactions? Knowing how much negativity they create, why do I keep emotionally reacting to people?

Because you take things personally, you only react emotionally when the situation has a particular meaning to you. Your thoughts create this meaning according to your psychological programming based on your past life experiences.

You may be sensitive to external judgments and criticisms. When someone says something you perceive as critical or dismissive, it can feel like an attack on your sense of self, leading you to take it personally. For example, when your partner asks you why you left your laptop on the kitchen counter, you may get offended because you feel it's a condescending remark toward you.

You may be naturally more empathetic or sensitive, which can lead you to feel and analyze the emotions and intentions of others intensely. This sensitivity usually creates an inherent desire to be liked and accepted. When you experience interactions threatening this acceptance, you may interpret them as personal judgments and mistakenly internalize them. For example, when one of your closest friends doesn't return your text about weekend plans, you may think that you did something wrong to them, and therefore, you're being distanced.

You may have insecurities and self-doubt that influence how you perceive certain situations. For example, you email the deck of slides to your boss and your team for an upcoming meeting. Then, your boss responds with a question, "Who prepared these slides?" You immediately take it personally, thinking that you made a big mistake. You perceive your boss' question as a negative reflection on you.

We can expand the above example to other occasions where your partner asks, "Who put the dark clothes with the white ones?" or "Who placed the wine glasses in the lower tray of the dishwasher?" You may have similar emotional reactions due to taking these questions and remarks as personal offenses.

Therefore, when interacting with others, it doesn't really matter whether a person has a particular attitude, tone, or facial expression. You have every right to take their actions, words, and approach personally. You hold the key to the meaning you project onto these people and situations and whether you let them trigger you.

But I naturally react to them because they offend me. Are you saying it's not their fault for triggering me?

It's not about whose fault it is. Emotional mastery involves fully owning your reactions by recognizing and understanding them deeply. It means acknowledging your thoughts and feelings without judgment, exploring their origins, and consciously choosing how to respond rather than being driven by automatic impulses. If you keep pointing fingers at others for triggering you, you may miss important information on why you interpret certain situations the way you do. Yes, others make you angry, upset, and frustrated, but what do they do precisely that elicits intense emotional reactions in you?

Look, you need emotions, whether they're positive or negative. Emotions activate your body. They can make you feel on top of the world with joy, love, gratitude, and happiness, and they can make you feel down and lost in despair or sadness. Emotional reactions are natural ways of responding to life's ups and downs.

At the same time, negative emotions are significantly pronounced when people don't respect your boundaries and don't do what you expect them to do. You experience intense emotional reactions when situations don't go how you want them to. Since you don't have control over the direction of your life, you always feel that you need to be on your toes to ward off threats to your comfort zone and carefully set boundaries.

When you live in that constant survival state, you try to find comfort by looking outside yourself for happiness and relying on others for positive emotions. That's why you keep blaming them when they trigger you. You hold them responsible for taking your joy away and making you unhappy. Of course, this creates extreme codependence in your relationship, eventually creating resentment for your partner becoming a source of drama between you.

You keep hoping that one day, your partner will change for the better or that something new will save your relationship and make you and your partner happy. Yet, these changes rarely take place. Even when they do, they don't last long. That's how you eventually lose hope and feel lost as to how to go on with your relationship.

Whenever you place your expectations, anticipations, and hopes in other people or on a set of circumstances, you set yourself up for disappointment by giving away your power. You place your happiness in their hands. Feeling powerless, you become more and more vulnerable and sensitive to what other people say or how they act around you. The relationship becomes shaky ground. That's why most of us live in constant anxiety and worry.

By becoming aware of your emotional reactions and understanding their cause, you start to balance the power dynamics between you and your partner. When you apply the first Power Step, Pause, you give yourself a chance to collect your thoughts and set clear boundaries that help you create more meaningful responses. A new paradigm begins to take place in your relationship through this subtle change in how you interact with your partner.

You're saying that people can still trigger me, but how I respond to them is up to me. And to regulate my emotional reactions, all I need to do is to become aware of them and understand why I'm emotionally reacting. Is that right?

That's precisely the point. This self-awareness and more profound understanding are the building blocks to achieving emotional mastery. However, they are not easy to attain, as the reasons you react are well hidden in the depths of your subconscious. Your automatic fight-or-flight defense mechanisms get activated only because of the special meaning you give to a trigger or whatever the other person does to you.

The moment you assign this interpretation of what's happening to you, your attention turns to others, and you start blaming them for what they're doing to you. In that moment, your subconscious takes control of your actions. In that state, you can only defend yourself against this person until you're energetically exhausted.

You can't break free from these destructive drama cycles without knowing why exactly you react to people. You require a substantial shift in your awareness. You need a deeper understanding of your subconscious and its fight-or-flight defense mechanisms. Without such expanded self-awareness, you can't override your automatic reactions.

But everything happens so quickly. How can I even grasp what's going on? Where do I begin to understand my programming?

Yes, the time between the trigger and the need to defend yourself is milliseconds. You don't have much time to understand what's going on. However, right in that time frame, even though it's a blink of an eye, you can access an incredible amount of information about yourself. You don't want to miss those moments revealing insights into your subconscious and why it's activating your fight-or-flight defense mechanisms.

Then the key question is, how does your subconscious reveal itself?

Through your emotional reactions.

If you'd like to know how your subconscious programming runs, then, you may want to pay attention to your emotional reactions.

However, where does your attention usually go when you're reacting?

Of course, on to the other person who has just triggered you. This is a natural consequence of being defensive.

When you're in that state of mind, there's no way you can pay attention to what's happening internally. That's why you go through the motions of your reactions without any awareness and understanding of why you're reacting. Always remember that self-knowledge is power. Without acquiring such valuable information about yourself, you stay under the tight control of your subconscious and end up unintentionally saying or doing things you later regret.

How can I catch myself mid-reaction? Maybe more like, how do I stop before going too far?

Learning to pause is probably the most challenging step in emotional mastery. It requires you to overcome your instinctive, subconscious fight-or-flight defense mechanisms.

At the same time, because it interrupts your automatic reaction, pausing is the most powerful step—without the ability to pause, there's no Power Method. The techniques described in this book help you develop this skill. Then, it's up to you how much you'd like to practice, which is directly correlated to how much you'd like to create better relationships.

Once you master how to pause, you experience a magical moment. You sense that time slows down and gives you space to apply the rest of the Power Steps consciously. When you have more time and feel more grounded, you expand your awareness and turn your reactions into proper responses. As a result, you use Communication Strategies more effectively, substantially creating positive outcomes in your relationships through meaningful interactions and deeper connections.

I understand the importance of learning to pause. How do I train myself to do that?

Emotional mastery is the ability to regulate your emotional reactions. To execute such a difficult task, you must pause and go against your instinctive fight-or-flight defense mechanisms. You must override nature. You can appreciate how difficult it is to achieve such levels. Hence, while trying to pause during a triggering event, be totally prepared to fail the first few times. As I mentioned earlier, you have less than a second between the trigger and your emotional reaction. It's tough to overcome that subconscious programming without any substantial training.

The following practice, your first Power Technique, is designed to help you learn to pause and slow down your emotional reactions and defensive actions enough to notice your emotions.

FIRST POWER TECHNIQUE: SQUARE BREATHING

Square Breathing is a simple yet profoundly effective breathing technique that helps you slow down your breathing, calm your mind, relax your body, and improve your focus. Its effectiveness comes from training your mind to concentrate on two things simultaneously: your breathing and the count of time.

This is how you practice this amazing breath technique and slowly get into the habit of remembering to pause when you're triggered and stressed.

First, inhale to a count of five. Hold your breath in as you count to five, and then exhale to a count of five. To complete the square, stop and hold, with your lungs empty, for another five counts. As you practice, imagine drawing a square with your breath, inhaling and exhaling at the same pace, and holding the air in or out of your lungs for the same count of five. When you complete the cycle, begin a new pattern with your next inhale.

This technique helps you become present by focusing your mind on two things: your breath and the count. As you count to five while you hold your breath, you calm your nervous system and decrease stress in your body, so subtle physical sensations become more noticeable. As a result, you'll feel an expansion of your inward-focused awareness, which is extremely important when emotionally reacting to triggers.

What kind of results should I expect when I practice Square Breathing?

Within a few days of starting a daily breath practice, you should notice a subtle shift in your awareness of where your attention goes. Wait and watch for that specific moment when you are in the middle of an emotional reaction. Catch yourself and notice what's happening and why you are getting triggered.

As you get more comfortable with this inward focus, which gives you space to identify your emotions, it gets easier and easier for you to be present during a trigger event and say, "Oh, I'm angry now," or, "Wow, I'm so frustrated with this person," or to ask yourself, "Why am I anxious all of a sudden?"

These questions and reflections are the first signs that you're taking back control of your emotional reactions from your subconscious and bringing more emotional awareness to your conscious mind.

What do I do after I pause?

Do you notice where your attention goes when you're triggered? I hope you start to realize how quickly your attention turns outward to others in those trigger events, where you take things personally and get defensive.

Once you achieve a level of proficiency in slowing down your reactions, you'll find yourself in a mental space to be able to turn your attention on yourself and apply your first Power Tool to notice your emotions.

FIRST POWER TOOL: I'M {THE EMOTION}

When practicing Square Breathing, you not only train your focus on two things at the same time but also learn to turn your attention inward to acknowledge what's happening to you internally. As a result, during a trigger event, you'll have the ability to become self-aware enough to acknowledge the emotion that you experience in that heated moment.

To reinforce this activity, the first Power Tool encourages you to pause to notice your emotions and say them out loud or at least to yourself. The simple phrase, "I'm {angry} right now," immediately turns your attention to what's happening internally. You don't necessarily need to share your emotions with others if doing so may not be safe initially. However, if you feel comfortable, please tell them what emotions you're experiencing at that moment without blaming them.

Why do I need to turn my attention inward and acknowledge my emotions?

Your emotions carry enormous information about you. Think of your emotions as the tip of an iceberg. There's so much going on underneath the surface. You have no idea because it's all in your subconscious. You pay so much attention to others and are too busy defending yourself that the chance to acquire self-knowledge passes in front of your eyes.

When your emotions erupt and you visibly get out of control, it is crucial to understand why you take these triggers personally. Here lies the difficulty: the only way to access that data is when you're in the middle of the trigger. You have to be grounded and present in the heat of the moment to watch what's happening internally and take a deeper look at what triggers your fight-or-flight defense mechanisms.

What kind of information or self-knowledge am I looking for behind my emotions?

Let's look at a real-life situation and go a little deeper to understand emotional reactions.

Ana reached out to me to find ways to improve her twelve-year marriage as she felt it was on the brink of falling apart. She was considering leaving her husband. In our first session, she complained about how her husband constantly criticized her no matter what she did. She would come home from work, a very demanding, high-flying job, and then go to the kitchen to prepare dinner.

When her husband got home, he would start commenting on how she was chopping the onions, how green bell peppers should be sliced, how much olive oil needed to be put in the pan, and so on. It drove Ana crazy. She had been passively silent about the constant criticism, but it had become unbearable lately. Just that week, when her husband put her down with a sarcastic comment for placing the wine glasses in the lower tray of the dishwasher, it was the last straw. She called me for help.

So, what's happening here? Why is Ana emotionally reacting to her husband?

The obvious answer is that her husband doesn't treat her well. Yes! Correct! No doubt.

At the same time, is there something else happening under the surface?

Remember that if you expect others to make you happy or modify or adjust their actions to behave how you want them to, you give your power to them. They don't have the consciousness or the awareness of what they're doing, so they won't change. They can't because they're not learning emotional mastery and doing their own deep personal work.

Let's look at what else is going on. How can Ana take her power back?

Before she decides to leave her husband, she can at least try to apply the 5-Step Power Method to empower herself and level the playing field by standing up to the verbal abuse she has been receiving.

Here are a series of questions I asked her to find out what was happening to her internally when she was emotionally reacting to her husband's comments. These questions will also give you some cues and insights into how to dive deep under the surface to figure out why "emotions are the tip of the iceberg" and what kind of information lies underneath them.

A. What trigger event did you just experience?
Her description: My husband constantly criticizes me for doing everything wrong. In his eyes, I don't seem to know anything.

B. What emotions are you experiencing?
Her emotions: I get angry, frustrated, and sad. I also feel resentful that I'm married to someone like him.

C. What creates these emotions?
Her thoughts: I think he enjoys putting me down. He feels superior. He's a perfectionist and minimizes my efforts.

D. Where do these thoughts come from?
Her feelings: I feel belittled. I feel not good enough. I feel less than. I feel worthless.

E. Have you felt these feelings before? Are they familiar to you from other situations in your life?
Her past: Yes, I feel patronized at work by my boss. He's part of the "old boys club," and they all look down on me as the only woman VP on the executive team. I also remember that when I was growing up, my dad was critical of me and wanted me to work harder and harder to get onto the varsity volleyball team in high school. I remember how embarrassing it was to hear him scream at me during games. I finally told him I would quit if he kept screaming in my games and training sessions. It created a lot of drama at home.

Now, how do you reflect on this conversation with Ana?

Can you see how her emotions, valid and justifiable for her situation, result from a much longer internal process? When you experience a trigger event, you can follow the thread of your emotions down into your thoughts and feelings. When you realize that your feelings are a common theme throughout your life, they qualify as your repressed fears.

Every time you take triggers personally, they have provoked those fears. They expose your vulnerability. That's how they take your happiness away. Once you learn what's underneath your emotions and understand why you react the way you do, you will be able to slow down enough to regulate your emotional reactions and reconsider your defensive actions.

What is the difference between "emotions" and "feelings"? We often use them interchangeably. Are they really different concepts?

Yes, they are. Even though we tend to treat these words to mean the same thing in everyday life, they are two different concepts for emotional mastery. It's essential to differentiate them and understand each to acquire the deep self-knowledge required to use the 5-Step Power Method against triggers most effectively.

Let me walk you through each definition and share some examples.

An emotion is an energy in motion—in other words, an e-motion. It's a charge that propels your body into action. Anger, anxiety, worry, sadness, jealousy, frustration, resentment, grief, regret, shame, and so on are all emotions that you experience as the result of a trigger event.

When someone triggers you, you sense your emotions as a charge. This energy shows up as an intense physical sensation in your body. It can manifest as tension, tightness, contractions, heaviness, or other palpable sensations. Once you slow down and manage to pause, you can inwardly focus on what's happening in your mind and body and collect all this self-knowledge you use to achieve emotional mastery.

Feelings, on the other hand, generate the narrative of your inner thoughts about a trigger event. In a way, your feelings make you take triggers personally. As a result, they inform your thoughts, which elicit an emotion in your body.

Some of the most common feelings I've seen over the years are not being good enough, not being recognized, being abandoned, being lonely, not being valued, being betrayed, being a failure, not being appreciated, and not being seen. You see how they differ from emotions like anger, frustration, sadness, anxiety, and worry.

This point is so important that I want to elaborate further. Feelings are your internal impressions, while thoughts are your mental commentary. For example, in Ana's situation above, her first thought is that her husband keeps putting her down. She doesn't question whether this is true—though, in this case, it is.

For the purposes of emotional mastery, we don't judge thoughts, positive or negative. We don't try to change them. We just observe them as they are. The thoughts are not the enemy. They are simply the narrative that subconscious programming assigns to a trigger event. Therefore, we don't fight with our thoughts; we get curious about them.

With that curiosity, we want to inquire how her husband's constant criticism makes her feel. In this case, she feels put down. She feels belittled. She feels not good enough. When we look deeper, we see these feelings remind her of past experiences with her dad, where he would yell at her and force her to do things better. She painfully travels back to her high school days and realizes how those experiences are the origins of her repressed fears.

Let's examine the sequence of how Ana experiences the trigger:

1. **The trigger happens.** Ana's husband tells her how to chop onions.

2. **Her repressed fears are triggered.** Subconsciously, her husband's criticism elicits past feelings related to situations where her dad made similar comments that made her feel not good enough, eventually becoming her repressed fear of not being good enough.

3. **Her feelings are provoked.** Ana's impression of the trigger event is that she feels not good enough, along with feeling put down, belittled, and unvalued.

4. **Her thoughts interpret the situation according to her feelings.** Ana thinks and perceives that her husband is criticizing her again, as he always does. Her subconscious fires up her fight-or-flight defense mechanisms.

5. **Her emotions are activated.** She's now angry at her husband for criticizing her and making that snarky comment.

Every time you experience a trigger event, you go through these five stages without knowing much about what's happening during stages two, three, and four since they occur within your subconscious. Yet these essential stages carry data—the self-knowledge about why you take triggers personally and, hence, emotionally react to others.

Interesting! Now, I'm curious about the difference between feelings and repressed fears? How do you differentiate them from each other?

Feelings only become repressed fears if and when they form a common, repeating theme throughout your life. In the example above, Ana does not feel good enough, which has come up consistently throughout her life. I bet she has been triggered many times by other people who made her feel that way over her lifetime beyond what she could recall.

When "feeling not good enough" is a common theme in her life, we qualify this impression as a repressed fear. This qualification is due to the fact that specific feeling is rooted in an emotional wound that she incurred in her past and has experienced throughout her life.

If a feeling is not a common theme in one's life, it is simply a feeling and not a repressed fear. In her specific case, we conclude that it is a repressed fear since it's a frequent feeling in her life that we can trace all the way to her childhood and high school years.

You, me, and everyone in the world have experienced dramatic, emotionally hurtful events in our past. Of course, the severity of trauma you experience may be different from others. At the same time, no matter what you experienced, the emotional pain was so hurtful that your subconscious suppressed these original feelings, and they became repressed fears that influenced your thought patterns, belief systems, and values. When suppressing all of this, your subconscious had only one goal in mind: to prevent you from experiencing these painful feelings again in the future.

What kind of painful feelings have you experienced in your past? Did your dad criticize you often, making you feel you were not good enough? Did your mom constantly scrutinize everything you did, which made you feel controlled? Was your older sibling the most popular or the smartest kid in high school, which made you feel overlooked? Did your younger sibling receive all the attention when they were newly born, which made you feel dismissed and not valued? Did any of your siblings, friends, or schoolmates bully you, which made you feel lonely, worthless, and low self-esteem?

Back then, you didn't necessarily have the tools to process these feelings right when you experienced them. As a result, these original unprocessed feelings or impressions have stayed with you. Your subconscious buried them into your psyche. Therefore, no matter how much you try to avoid experiencing these painful moments, you keep running into people and situations in your relationships that perpetuate and intensify those feelings and corresponding repressed fears you don't want to experience again.

The only way to break this cycle is to confirm that these feelings exist and accept that they are part of your subconscious. Once you learn about them, the trick is to bring that awareness to your consciousness when you're emotionally reacting to someone. That's emotional mastery. Before, all you knew was that you emotionally reacted because others offended you. But now, you better understand that you react because you have unprocessed, raw, repressed fears, and others trigger them.

Therefore, no matter how much your subconscious fires up its fight-or-flight defense mechanisms, as long as your repressed fears stay unprocessed and buried within your thought patterns, belief systems, and values, you keep running into people and situations that trigger you and elicit emotional reactions.

I understand from this that no matter how much I emotionally react, others will not change. They only trigger me because I haven't processed my repressed fears. Well then, can you tell me how to process them so I don't get triggered anymore?

You're correct that defensive reactions don't allow you to process your repressed fears. Nothing will change. No matter how much you get angry and frustrated with your spouse, kids, colleagues, friends, or parents, raise your voice at them, gossip about them, or stop talking to them, nobody will change how they interact with you. Soon after, they will trigger you again and keep you in those destructive drama cycles.

When you pay more attention to what's going on internally during these trigger events, you soon realize that it's not just your spouse or kids who make you feel this way but also your boss, your sister, your brother, your mom, your dad, and some of your friends who inflict similar feelings of emotional hurt in you.

If you want to stop taking triggers personally and eventually rise above them, you must change how you respond to them. In other words, if you want others to change, you change how you react to them. This shift from typical reactions to conscious responses fundamentally helps you achieve emotional mastery. Once you make the Power Method and its Communication Strategies your second nature, you experience a subtle, surprising, yet strong improvement in your interactions with others.

When your subconscious runs your life, you stay behind thick, tall walls to protect your heart. You have every right to do so because you don't want to be emotionally vulnerable again. However, pushing people away because you don't trust them unintentionally creates a "me vs. them" attitude. Of course, when you do that, people get triggered by you—because of their own repressed fears. As a result, everybody walks around with closed hearts, creating more distance from each other and preventing them from forming deep, meaningful relationships.

You can only close this gap by opening your heart, becoming aware of your repressed fears, and learning about their origins. In that open, vulnerable state, you can embrace and relive your past in the present moment. This time, though, you can take conscious actions. Instead of ignoring your feelings, you can get out of your victim state and use appropriate Communication Strategies to claim your power and set healthier boundaries.

When you face your repressed fears through the Power Method and its Communication Strategies, you realize the deeper meaning of your current relationships. When you reflect on how your past affects your present life, everything starts to make sense to you. Right at that moment, you begin to shift from reaction to response and experience triggers with less intensity and less frequency. Taking this first step—Pause—is the telltale sign that you're on your way to emotional mastery and the path to happiness.

I've been practicing Square Breathing, and I've started noticing my emotions when triggered. What should I do next?

You're ready to deploy your first Communication Strategy. When you gain the ability to pause in the midst of an emotional reaction, not only do you have access to your emotions and what's happening internally but also, you seize an invaluable opportunity to change your reactions. The more you practice square breathing, the quicker you can switch to a different response.

The trick is to take control of your awareness and use the slowing time to choose an action consciously or to do something that you haven't done before against similar triggers. The purpose of going out of your typical reactions and instigating a new, never-before action is to shake things up a little bit and confuse your automatic fight-or-flight defense mechanisms.

In a way, you become a two-year-old toddler and get to throw "terrible two" tantrums; the only difference this time is that you're going against your subconscious and no longer against your parents. To honor this disobedient and defiant behavior, I called the first Communication Strategy "Doing the Opposite."

FIRST COMMUNICATION STRATEGY: DOING THE OPPOSITE

I hope it's clear from your own experience that no matter what your subconscious, automatic defensive actions are, you soon find yourself in the same situation, watching the other person do the same thing to trigger you. They don't wake up every day with the goal of triggering you. On the contrary, your partner already forgot the discussion and doesn't quite understand why you take their actions personally. Therefore, there's no point in explaining or asking them to change. You can't expect different results if you react to them the same way you always do. The only way to create change in your interactions with others is to change the way you respond to them.

Once you develop the ability to pause, there's no better time to start switching your responses to change things up. You want to shock the subconscious that has been in charge of your life for a long time. With the Doing the Opposite strategy, you display disobedience and send a strong message to your subconscious that you are no longer abiding by its fight-or-flight defense mechanisms. To stand by your commitment, instead of giving in to your typical emotional reactions, start consciously altering them to something totally different from before.

To execute your first Communication Strategy, you need to be creative. I encourage you to fill out the Daily Review at the end of every day. During that exercise, you can pre-meditate on a similar trigger that may happen the next day and prepare yourself to respond differently.

For example, if you usually react to people or situations by raising your voice, try lowering your voice this time. If you leave the room and avoid conflict, this time, stay in the room and face the tricky interaction a little longer. If you've rolled your eyes in the past, try leaving the room or speaking up instead.

The important thing is that you are taking control of your subconscious. Now, you're on the steering wheel and ready to decide how to respond. Just focus on experimenting with various responses and be playful and curious about how much change you can bring in your responses and how it impacts your interactions with others.

How do I apply the Doing the Opposite strategy to a real-life scenario?

Let's go through an example of how this might work. Let's say you wake up on a Saturday morning, and your spouse tells you, "Why did you leave the dishes in the sink last night? I thought we talked about this. You need to put them away before you go to bed. I don't want to see a pile of dirty plates in the sink when I wake up. The kitchen smells like garbage."

If you don't have emotional mastery, your spouse's words could undoubtedly make you respond without thinking and start a dispute.

But since we're practicing a strategy, you're going to do something else instead. In the moment you feel triggered, pause and notice what kind of emotions you're experiencing.

Is it anger? Resentment? Frustration?

Then, internally acknowledge that emotion: I'm angry, resentful, or frustrated. Whatever comes up, pause, notice, and recognize.

Next, consider how you usually react to your spouse. Maybe you raise your voice and tell them to stop bugging you, and you blame them for bullying you and being on your case all the time. Perhaps you roll back into bed and quietly wonder how long you can take this abuse and what you did wrong to have ended up with a spouse like this. Maybe you start to explain how the neighbors stayed too long, and it got late, and you were tired, and you thought you could take care of the dishes today. Maybe you roll your eyes and ask them why they need to share all that at 8:30 on a Saturday morning. Maybe you get up, slam the bedroom door, and get into the shower while yelling how they always make a big deal of nothing.

Which of the options above is your typical reaction, and how can you change it to something else you haven't done before? Consider the following.

If you raise your voice, can you be quiet?

If you go back to bed, can you speak up?

If you try to explain, can you roll your eyes?

If you roll your eyes, can you raise your voice?

If you ignore them, can you try to explain?

If you successfully change your reaction to something else, you have executed the Doing the Opposite strategy perfectly. Feel free to change things up and consciously try different approaches when emotionally reacting to triggers. As you can see, you are still reacting and not quite responding to triggers. The first Communication Strategy is, by design, challenging you to come up with different reactions and, if available, other responses. When you are more aware of the moment, you can change how you deal with a trigger, even though you're still emotionally reacting.

I'm concerned that I might escalate the conflict and cause more trouble in my life. When I apply this Doing the Opposite strategy, will I face difficulties or pushback from others?

Yes, until you strike assertive, non-defensive energy, you can expect some pushback from others whenever you apply a new Communication Strategy, regardless of the strategy.

Do you know why?

Because every new strategy requires higher levels of self-awareness from you. This means that when you apply the second Power Step, Observe Your Thoughts, and its corresponding Communication Strategy, you need to have more awareness and a deeper understanding of yourself. Similarly, the third Power Step will require more than the second, the fourth more than the third, and so on.

Until you reach such expanded awareness and higher levels of consciousness, your execution may fall short, as your response may not carry the necessary assertiveness and power to succeed. As a result, it may trigger the other person who triggered you in the first place.

Also, think about the other person's position. They're not studying emotional mastery and are accustomed to your typical defensive reactions. The moment you start mixing things up, they get confused. They sense something is up with you but can't tell what. That uncertainty makes them suspicious and more defensive. That's also when you get some initial pushback on your Communication Strategies.

The bottom line is, yes, you'll face resistance from others when applying new strategies. I call this phenomenon "waves of resistance." From what I've seen over the years with my clients, it usually occurs multiple times, but the most I've ever counted was five waves, which occurred on rare occasions. That means that over the course of one conversation, the other person comes back defensively five times when you're trying to apply a new strategy. The name of the game is to be patient. Stay on course and learn from your experiments.

By the way, let me clarify an important point. Power and assertiveness should not be mistaken for force and aggression. In the context of emotional mastery, power means integrity that keeps you within your personal boundaries without crossing into others'. When you offend others, you've crossed their boundaries and provoked their repressed fears.

On the other hand, assertiveness is rightfully and peacefully enforcing your boundaries in a considerate and careful way, again without infringing upon others. In any situation, if you are combative, you'll be encroaching on others' boundaries, making them defensive. They will certainly come back and offend you, creating more conflict and hostility. In other words, power comes from within, while force is an outward phenomenon.

So, I guess I should expect some pushback. What shall I do when these "waves of resistance" happen to me?

Try to be patient when using your Communication Strategies. Keep in mind that you're going to be a little wobbly in the beginning. It's unknown territory for you. You're going against your known, standard, automatic, subconscious fight-or-flight defense mechanisms. Keep your expectations low and aim for one successful execution of Doing the Opposite out of a hundred tries. I call this the "one-out-of-one hundred" rule. Fail as often as necessary through trial and error, but never give up. Just one successfully executed Communication Strategy will give you self-assurance and change your life. That's why I say master your emotions, master your life. But it's easier said than done, for sure!

The benefit of starting with the Doing the Opposite strategy is that it changes the flow of your conversations and interactions. Many clients come back to me with stories about how something new and unexpected happens every time they do it. This happens when you're no longer defensive and desperately trying to protect yourself but instead opening yourself up with more courage and power. You're showing up for the moment and rising to the occasion.

I recently had a client, let's call her Sherry, who shared an interesting Doing the Opposite episode with her fifteen-year-old son, who was learning how to drive. Sherry goes with her son in the car to teach him how to drive and show him what to pay attention to. Every time they go out, they come back arguing because Sherry can't help but emotionally react and make critical comments like, "You have to stop for three seconds," or "Why aren't you paying attention?" or "You can't do this; otherwise, you're going to fail the test." These outbursts happen over and over again. Finally, her son asks her, "Mom, why are you so angry at me? I hate going on these drives with you! You're so overly critical."

Sherry is devastated. Her son has a driving test in a few weeks, and she is nervous that he isn't good enough to pass the test. On top of that, most of his friends have already gotten their licenses. As a mother, she wants to protect him from possible failure and humiliation among his friends. At the same time, she knows that if she reacts to him again the way she has, it will turn into another argument, affect his confidence, and possibly make him fail his driving test. It may even damage her relationship with him, and he will refuse to go on these test rides with her.

However, practice still has to happen, so they schedule another drive. This time, Sherry decides to apply Doing the Opposite. And, inevitably, the moment comes. Her son, as usual, doesn't pay attention at a stop sign and comes to a rolling stop. Sherry quietly watches him. Despite being frustrated, she exerts every ounce of willpower to remain silent. Right at that moment, Sherry remembers her Square Breathing—she inhales for a count of five, holds her breath for five, exhales for five, and lastly, holds her breath out for five. After just one round, she feels so much calmer and in control of her reactions.

The rest of the ride is pretty uneventful. They both stay quiet until they get home. Her son goes straight to his room and does his thing. As it gets closer to dinner time, her son comes out of his room and joins Sherry and her husband in the living room. He approaches my client with a serious face and says, "I really appreciate you not criticizing my driving today, Mom. I felt more relaxed, and it was the most enjoyable ride we've been on together. I think I'm ready for the test. I feel I can pass. Thank you for your support and trust in me."

Of course, Sherry melts when she receives her son's appreciation, and she also feels encouraged by his increased confidence in himself. In a state of semi-shock, she can't find the words to say anything in response to her son's gesture. But she manages to hug him with tears in her eyes. The day after this moment of deep connection, her son invites my client for one last practice run. Sherry jumps into the car without knowing why they are on the road again. Her curiosity is fulfilled at the end of their drive when she realizes in awe that her son has fully stopped at all stop signs and paid attention to oncoming traffic before crossing each intersection.

I guess Sherry broke free from her destructive drama cycle and experienced a positive result. Can you explain a little bit more what really happens in these situations, maybe by sharing a few more examples?

These kinds of remarkable outcomes happen when you override your subconscious programming. However, when you are reactive and act out of your fight-or-flight defense mechanisms, you come across as "offensive" to the other person. That's why you end up getting into fruitless arguments, as everyone keeps defending their position and offending each other.

Every defense is an offense. When you defend yourself, you don't recognize the other person. You're worried about your own position. You're adamant about how great and true your opinions are. You're simply too attached to winning arguments or imposing your opinions onto others. Such acts ignore the other person. When you fail to see, hear, or acknowledge them, you practically dismiss them. Of course, this dismissal offends them and elicits their own emotional reaction, which kicks off a sequence of unproductive back-and-forth arguments. In the end, you end up creating nothing but drama.

The first Communication Strategy, Doing the Opposite, is designed to break this vicious cycle of fruitless arguments. Sherry executes this strategy by staying quiet and giving her son some space instead of trying to control his actions. Hence, his response to her also becomes non-defensive. And they reconcile and settle their case.

Here are three scenarios for you to review and study. Pay attention to how the new response replaces the old reaction. Try to visualize yourself in similar situations in your own life and reflect on how you could respond to them by pausing and applying the Doing the Opposite strategy.

Scenario One

The Trigger: Sue complains that her husband is constantly on his phone, distracted as he seemingly checks, reads, and responds to his work emails. Sometimes, she sees him texting others as well. Recently, even though she isn't supposed to do it, she gets his phone and types in his password to check out who he's been chatting with. She immediately sees that he has been having conversations with several people she doesn't know. She recognizes the names of a few women from her husband's sailing club. As she looks through their messages, she's taken aback by how much excitement they have when talking about the details of their future adventures. Their tone is overly friendly to the point of outright flirtation.

Emotions: Sue experiences anger, sadness, and frustration.

Old Reaction: She usually stays quiet and says nothing when her husband upsets her. Most of the time, she pretends nothing happened.

New Response: After learning the Doing the Opposite strategy, Sue pauses amid her trigger response and decides to face her husband instead of pretending she doesn't know anything. She asks him who he's been messaging. He claims that some are former colleagues and a few are sailing companions. Sue raises her voice a little bit (even though she's shaking from nerves because this is the first time she's doing this in her marriage) and collects herself enough to say, "Well, I have a problem with your chatting spending time with people I've never met, and you've never mentioned. How can I trust you? It's disrespectful to our marriage, and you should be ashamed of yourself." Then, she leaves the room and goes to the bedroom to cry. She slams the door—a first! She executes her Doing the Opposite so well that her husband later knocks gently on their bedroom door, comes into the room, and apologizes to her.

Scenario Two

The Trigger: Matt and Claire have two kids, Hanna and Rana, who are eight and eleven years old. Claire is the vice president at a large organization, which is extremely demanding, while Matt is a stay-at-home dad. However, he struggles with parenting duties as their daughters frequently disrespect him and undermine his authority. This dynamic triggers him on a daily basis. He doesn't know how to deal with them and struggles to get them to comply with his requests. Even simple things like brushing their teeth before bed or putting on their shoes before they leave for school in the morning become a battlefield of egos.

Emotions: Matt is frustrated with the kids and at his wits' end. He's constantly on edge and occasionally has angry outbursts, which irritates Claire and strains their marriage.

Old Reaction: Most mornings, Matt tries to ensure the kids get to school comfortably, so he rushes around to prepare their lunches and gather bags and jackets while the kids take their time getting ready. When the time comes to leave, Matt usually realizes they are behind schedule and begins yelling at them to hurry them out of the door so they're not late for class. After dropping them off, he comes home, exhausted and drenched in sweat. Then he crashes into bed and takes a nap for half an hour.

New Response: One morning, Matt decides to use the Doing the Opposite strategy. Instead of rushing around, Matt asks the kids to prepare everything for school themselves. Initially, they ignore him and go back to bed, refusing to follow Matt's instructions. Usually, Matt would lose his temper. But this time, he pauses, goes to the kitchen, and tries Square Breathing. After a few deep breaths, he calms down. He returns to their bedrooms and tells them they have half an hour to get ready. He emphasizes teamwork and being on time. Matt also adds that he cares for them, and while he does want them to be punctual, he's okay with facing the consequences if they are late, and they should be, too.

His caring nonattachment to the outcome makes the kids think for themselves and begrudgingly take responsibility for their actions. They unwillingly start picking up a few things here and there. Matt goes with the flow, not worrying about the time, and drops them off after the class starts, letting them experience tardiness. They get a warning from their teachers, and that night, Matt and the kids discuss what happened. Matt asks the kids for their opinions about what they must do next. Both Hanna and Rana offer input, deciding to prepare everything the night before so they aren't late again.

The kids are surprised by Matt's inclusion of them in the decision-making process. They don't understand what's happening, but participating in the morning routine encourages them to speak up. Since everything is prepared the previous evening, they ask if they can skip breakfast and stay in bed for an extra ten minutes. Matt immediately wants to reject the idea but decides to follow the Doing the Opposite strategy and gets curious about what will happen tomorrow morning. He okays the kids' request as long as they pack a protein bar to eat on the way to school. As a result, the kids enjoy changing up the routine and collaborating with their dad. In the end, the lingering tardiness problem resolves itself by using a different Communication Strategy.

Scenario Three

The Trigger: Rebecca feels like she walks on eggshells around her in-laws, who seem to never care about what she has to say. They ignore her no matter what she does. Of course, this attitude intimidates her and makes her feel like a stranger in her own house. She has tried to talk to her husband, Rick, about it, but he doesn't see her side and tells her not to exaggerate. The situation is so bad that she takes anti-anxiety pills when they visit. As a result, she usually sits calmly in the corner with dampened emotions as a way of avoiding conversation. The in-laws are about to make another visit next month, and Rebecca can feel her skin crawling with enormous anxiety and stress.

Emotions: Rebecca experiences all sorts of anxiety, stress, overwhelm, and powerlessness, as well as a sense of sadness because her husband doesn't see her point of view.

Old Reaction: Even though she tries to avoid interacting with her in-laws, she gives in to the pressure to perform in a certain way to meet their expectations and spend a lot of time with them every time they visit. She tries to please them by catering to what they want, hoping they'll appreciate her efforts. Despite her best attempts, they always find a way to dismiss her, and she again finds herself withdrawing, getting bitter, and feeling exhausted.

New Response: This time, Rebecca decides to change her approach to break her destructive drama cycles with her in-laws. She mentally prepares herself to apply the Doing the Opposite strategy by consciously pausing and deciding to do less to impress them. For example, one night, instead of cooking for her in-laws, she suggests to Rick that they take everyone to their favorite restaurant.

Another day, instead of feeling obligated to spend time with her in-laws, she pauses and applies the Doing the Opposite strategy, booking some self-care appointments. She schedules a massage, gets her nails done, and meets up with a friend for coffee. She gives herself much-needed time and space.

When she executes her Doing the Opposite strategy and gives herself that much-needed time and space, surprisingly, she feels less of a need to withdraw. Their dismissing comments about her and how she does things around the house don't trigger her as intensely as before.

Feeling the positive shift in her interactions with her in-laws, she starts to enjoy her time around them. The more she pauses, the more opposite actions she takes. She goes on a walk in a nearby park. She leisurely sits at a café for a tasty cappuccino and time with her favorite book. The more she allocates time to herself, the more positive interactions she experiences with her husband's parents. Surprisingly, they all start to get along well, and her in-laws' future visits never become a source of anxiety anymore.

JOURNAL ENTRY FOR WEEK ONE

For the next seven days, make a journal entry at the end of each day as part of your Daily Review to capture the most intense trigger event that occurred. Do this review by answering the following questions:

1. What was the trigger event?
2. What emotions did you experience?
3. How did you feel when you paused?
4. What was your old reaction?
5. What was your new response?

DAILY CHECKLIST FOR WEEK ONE

1. Have you paused and noticed your emotions during a trigger event?

2. Have you practiced Square Breathing and become more present?

3. Have you internally acknowledged emotions with "I'm {the emotion}"?

4. Have you used the Doing the Opposite strategy?

CHAPTER THREE

OBSERVING THE UNSEEN

Thoughts that Spark our Emotions

In an ideal world, emotional mastery would be part of our education system from an early age. But here we are, figuring it out in our adult years, trying our best not to get tangled in those subconscious fight-or-flight defense mechanisms that lead us straight into never-ending destructive drama cycles.

To break free from the old conflict-ridden relationship patterns, we must dig deeper into our subconscious and understand what's driving these conflicts and our emotional reactions. While we feel emotions on the surface, they're often shaped by more profound, hidden thoughts that influence our automatic fight-or-flight defense mechanisms. As a result, we act like robots, subconsciously responding to these thoughts without even realizing it.

So, how do we change that? By hitting pause and only then observing the thoughts that spark our emotions. This is where the second Power Step comes in: Observe. By staying present and tuning into these underlying thoughts, we can start to make sense of our emotional reactions and take control back from our subconscious. This awareness can help us chart a path toward living more consciously and making mindful choices that will keep drama away from our relationships.

What underlying thoughts do I need to observe to understand my emotional reactions?

At this point in your journey, you've probably noticed that your thoughts influence how you interpret different situations, often making things feel personal when they might not be. You now realize that's exactly why you react emotionally to others. These reactions are usually tied to underlying fears and insecurities tucked away in our subconscious.

The exciting part of your journey toward emotional mastery is learning to unravel this programming and what your subconscious has been hiding. All the answers you seek are actually in thought forms waiting to be revealed to your consciousness. Your thoughts are the bridge that you need to cross to reach into the depths of your subconscious. Therefore, by understanding your deep-seated thought patterns, you'll start to see what lies beneath your emotions and get a better view of why certain things push your buttons.

To demonstrate this concept, let's look at what Henry, one of my clients, experiences during a family dinner a few days before our session.

Henry and his family are sitting around the table when his wife, Laurie, makes a snarky comment in front of their two children about how Henry sleeps in on the weekends and how the whole family wastes the day because of him. Right there. Boom! His wife's comments hit him like a ton of bricks. He gets triggered. What do you think he experiences as an emotion?

Immediate anger.

Everyone around the dining table senses Henry's anger. His face turns red.

We know that anger is an emotion—the visible tip of the subconscious. What lies underneath?

To go deeper and understand what's happening internally, Henry pauses and starts to observe his thoughts. When his wife makes a comment about him being lazy on the weekends, Henry immediately thinks, *My wife is ridiculing me in front of my kids! She never respects me. No matter what I do, she doesn't appreciate me. I'm doing everything around the house, working hard to provide for the family, taking everyone on vacation, and caring for everybody's problems. Why is she picking on me? So what's the problem when I try to catch up on some sleep on weekend mornings? I'm exhausted. Why can't she understand me?*

Of course, these thoughts race through Henry's mind at a thousand miles an hour. But he does his best to step back from the situation and observe what's happening in his mind. He realizes he thinks his wife doesn't appreciate him, doesn't respect him, and doesn't value him when she carelessly puts him down in front of the kids. Do Henry's thoughts reflect the reality of the situation? Is he wrong about what his wife thinks about him? Should he not have these thoughts?

No, no, not at all. Here's a quick tip: respect your thoughts as they are. Whether true or not, your thoughts reflect what's going on in your subconscious programming and are shaped by your repressed fears. They're your reality. That's why I mentioned earlier that you don't want to turn negative thoughts into positive ones. If you do, you'll lose valuable insights into your subconscious programming and miss the chance to go deeper. Therefore, try to avoid questioning the reality of your thoughts. Take them at face value and try not to judge them.

Whether Henry's wife thinks of him this way or that way is irrelevant. Henry's thoughts reflect his internal reality. And what his wife says about Henry is based on her own judgments or projections, which come from her thoughts of how she sees her husband. Ideally, since she's triggered by her husband's lack of energy on the weekends, she may want to understand her subconscious programming to uncover why she feels the need to embarrass him. Again, no one is at fault here. Both Henry and his wife are lost in their thoughts, which are merely the projections of their repressed fears that show up in their subconscious fight-or-flight defense mechanisms.

Can you imagine that one day, you might observe your thoughts naturally without evaluating them? Can you just allow yourself to experience the negative thoughts fully? Can you sense how mastering your emotions becomes possible when you resist the temptation to defend yourself? Can you go toe-to-toe against your fight-or-flight defense mechanisms and become freer from the subconscious programming that creates all the drama in your life?

By expanding your self-awareness and accepting all thoughts, negative or positive, without any artificial influence, you create a greater mental space and understanding of yourself to consciously choose more powerful responses to triggers and eventually break free from your destructive drama cycles.

Everything is happening so fast. How can I train myself not to get lost in my thoughts and observe them properly to create that space?

You might have already experienced how difficult it is to pause to notice your emotions and observe your thoughts during a trigger event. However, you might have also sensed that it's that moment where you need to take control back from your subconscious. That's precisely when you need to slow down the time to calmly observe the activity in your mind to get to the bottom of your subconscious programming.

Your particular training to accomplish this task is your next Power Technique, designed to sharpen your focus for longer periods to create a larger mental space where it gets easier to observe the busyness of your mind without getting lost in it.

SECOND POWER TECHNIQUE: SELF-OBSERVATION MEDITATION

This technique is not your typical meditation practice. In other meditation techniques, the goal is often to rid oneself of negative, intrusive, or cluttered thoughts and relax the mind. But in this meditation, you practice taking control of your attention and not pushing your thoughts away.

Objectively witnessing how your subconscious elicits your emotional reactions creates a new mental presence of mind, empowering you to take control of your actions. You're basically developing a new skill to regain your power without changing anything in your subconscious programming. Without forcing any artificial reprogramming or using positive thought reinforcements, your awareness naturally expands, helping you process your repressed fears at a deeper level.

The self-observation technique, in other words, is a mental practice that improves your ability to step back from a situation and witness it from a distance with detachment and indifference. This phenomenon happens when your consciousness becomes the third-party witness and starts to observe the actions of the subconscious. This practice allows you to slow down your thoughts, creating the expanded awareness and mental space you need to choose your responses consciously.

How do you practice this powerful technique?

Start by choosing a location where you won't be interrupted while practicing, then set a timer. If you're new to these types of meditations, you might want to start with just three minutes. Yes, just three minutes a day will be enough to train yourself to take over your attention and focus. Of course, you can add more time later when you feel more comfortable with the process.

Sit on a comfortable chair with your knees at a ninety-degree angle and your feet flat on the floor. Your back, neck, and head should be aligned. If the chair has a back, move forward toward the center of the chair so that your back doesn't rest on it; otherwise, you may get too comfortable and slouch or even fall asleep. If you have to lean your back on the chair, that's okay too, but in that case, keep your back straight to help create a sense of presence. Your goal should be to relax as much as possible while maintaining an erect posture without being rigid or strained.

Place your hands on your lap, one on top of the other, palms up, fingers pointing in opposite directions, without interlocking. Next, bring your thumbs together, creating a circle, and let them softly touch each other on their meaty tips while being careful not to press too hard. In this pose, you create a basket where your palms represent the container and your thumbs the handle. Let your arms relax.

Now, take a deep breath in, and as you exhale, close your eyes. Keep your mouth closed and breathe naturally. Bring your focus to the light touch of your thumbs, noticing the tangible, physical sensation that your thumbs create. Hold your attention there as long as you can.

Only seconds after focusing on your thumbs, your thoughts will try to distract your attention. Initially, you won't even notice when this happens. You will softly drift into daydreaming. Soon, you'll find yourself swimming in mind chatter: your thoughts, stories, interpretations of what happened today, plans for the evening, worries, and emotional reactions to this person or that situation will all show up.

Well, no worries. Your practice begins right in that chaos. It's okay if you're lost in your thoughts, frustrated by the overwhelming activity, or your body starts to itch. It's okay if you can't even sit still for thirty seconds.

Simply try to observe what's going on and what you're thinking and feeling at that moment. In other words, just pay attention to your mind's busyness or your body's discomfort. That's basically what self-observation meditation is training you for: to catch yourself while subconsciously reacting and regain your awareness by taking control over your attention. Over time, through some patience and consistent practice, you *will* create the mental space you need to regulate your emotional reactions.

When you want to finish your practice, take a deep breath in, and then softly exhale while slowly opening your eyes and releasing your hands and thumbs. Check in with yourself. How are you feeling now?

I recommend practicing self-observation meditation at least once a day. To improve your technique, you can join me on Episode 42 of the *Rise 2 Realize Podcast*, where I guide you step-by-step through this practice.

I've found over the years that the best time for me is right after I wake up—before diving into the busyness of my day. Feel free to experiment with different times throughout the day to figure out what works best for you.

You may also want to try practicing twice a day—once in the morning and once before you go to bed at night—or slipping in a one-minute practice here and there throughout the day—between meetings, errands, or meals—or even when you're waiting for the red light to turn green.

You may have grand expectations that this practice will change your life immediately. Although it will positively impact how you regulate your emotional reactions, changes may not happen tomorrow or next week. Over the last fifteen years, I've taught this practice to thousands of people with varying results. All of them went through the following five phases to get the best results:

Phase 1: The first phase is noticing how busy your mind is. Simply try to acknowledge as many thoughts going through your mind as possible. It's absolutely okay to get lost in your thoughts and not remember what you were thinking about.

Phase 2: The second phase is about catching yourself thinking. The key question here is, "Can you notice yourself while daydreaming?" It's tricky, isn't it? You need to step outside of yourself to observe yourself. You can only do this when you take control of where your focus is.

Phase 3: The third phase is about acknowledging the last thought you had before taking control of your attention. This action is like putting your hand into a pond full of fish and catching one, then acknowledging it. Is it salmon, trout, seabass, or tuna? After determining what kind of fish you've caught, release it back into the pond. Similarly, with Self-Observation Meditation, you want to acknowledge your thoughts and then let them stay where they are, hanging untouched and ineffective. Simply observe that thought and let it go.

Phase 4: The fourth phase is about bringing your full attention to your thumbs. Once you've taken control of your attention, consciously place it on the physical sensation that your thumbs create. Direct your focus from thoughts to the sense of your touch consciously with both your mind and your body. For example, you might say to yourself, *I'm shifting my focus to the sensation my thumbs create.*

Phase 5: The fifth phase is about trying to focus on the sensation as long as possible. Once you connect with it, try to feel the sensation, stay with the sensation, and be the sensation. Practice "being the sensation" with your body, not your mind. Try to lose yourself in your focus as you become the sensation.

You'll likely feel a shift in your consciousness when you reach that moment. You'll experience an inner calmness, a state of tranquility everywhere in your body. Ride that connection with your higher levels of awareness until your thoughts return to your attention and drag you back into your mind. Then, repeat the process to find your thumbs again.

What do I do with the thoughts I observe?

Before I answer your question and share the second Power Tool with you, let's review the mechanics of subconscious programming again, this time in more detail, to truly understand why you take triggers personally:

1. The trigger event happens to you.

2. Your subconscious programming decides some of the details of what's happening now are similar to the original event that caused repressed fears.

3. Your repressed fears provoke your feelings and create impressions of similar feelings that you experienced in that past traumatic event.

4. Your feelings activate your thoughts through subconscious programming consisting of thought patterns, belief systems, and values. This programming states that if "ABC" happens, it means "XYZ." In other words, your programming discerns how you need to experience this trigger event and gives you cues on why it's a provocation and why you should take it personally.

5. The trigger becomes a threat to your vulnerability. Right there and then, your subconscious fight-or-flight defense mechanisms take control of the situation, eliciting your emotions and creating the impetus for your body to defend itself. As a result, your typical defensive actions, whether aggressive, passive-aggressive, or passive, are activated against the person that triggered you.

This sequence is basically the map for you to better understand where your emotional reactions and defensive actions come from. The big hang-up or hindrance within the disciplines of psychology is not differentiating the energies between emotions and feelings. As we discussed earlier, they are two completely different concepts, and without separating them and treating them differently, you can't dive deep enough into your subconscious programming to untangle its interpretation of every trigger. Hence, investigating your observed thoughts becomes even more critical, as you want to go below the surface to fully understand your subconscious programming.

SECOND POWER TOOL: REVERSE ENGINEERING WITH "WHAT IF—SO WHAT" QUESTIONS

Get your scuba gear ready; we're diving in! When an emotion is the tip of the iceberg, and it is what you and everyone see, the thoughts that ignite it are the unseen elements of the subconscious. They're always there in your mind, but you don't pay attention to them. When they get too loud, negative, or disturbing, you try to push them away, hoping that the "out of sight, out of mind" principle applies to your thoughts.

Thoughts are like dogs. When you run away from them, they'll chase you. The only way you can tame your thoughts is to turn around and face them. Make the unseen seen. Once you start to observe them, they become visible. Through this enhanced access to your thoughts, you can now dive deeper into the depths of your subconscious.

If emotions come from thoughts, then what's underneath thoughts? Feelings!

How do you get from thoughts to feelings? Through the process of reverse engineering.

You can use this simple yet profound tool to challenge your thoughts by asking a series of "What If—So What" Questions until you hone in on meaningful feelings that resonate within you.

To help you with this process, every time you challenge a thought, also ask yourself, "How does this trigger event make me feel?" Whenever you force yourself to answer this question with a feeling (not with an emotion), you'll face the real culprits underneath your thoughts.

When applying the reverse engineering tool, the key success factor is differentiating feelings from emotions. If you keep answering the questions with emotions, you'll be caught in a whirlpool and unable to go further or dive deeper. Therefore, try to pay attention to how an e-motion acts as an "energy" that activates the body into "motion." In contrast, a feeling is an impression, i.e., an internal imprint in your subconscious that creates defensive thoughts.

In the recent trigger event we have just reviewed, Henry is angry (an emotion) because he thinks, *My wife doesn't appreciate me!* This thought is the starting point for the reverse engineering process:

Henry will challenge his thought and ask, *What if my wife doesn't appreciate me, so what? How does that make me feel?*

He answers with another thought. *Well, she never sees what I do for the family and then thinks I'm lazy, sitting around all day and twirling my thumbs. Enough of that!!*

He pauses as he realizes his emotions are being triggered. He closely observes these thoughts and then rechallenges them. *What if she thinks I'm lazy, so what? How does this make me feel?*

Henry first answers this question with an emotion, *It pisses me off!* Then, he remembers that if he stays with emotions (anger and frustration), he'll continue floating on the surface and not delve deep enough to understand his profound feelings about the situation.

He tries again, and this time, he answers the question with his feelings: I feel not seen, not important, and not worthy of her love.

When he reaches the depths of his feelings, he gets emotional. But it's no longer anger. He experiences sadness. He realizes right then what he has been hiding for his entire life: *that he feels worthless.*

Memories flood his mind. As a child, his mom rarely appreciated him when he did things for her. He also realizes he'd never felt understood or seen by his dad when he accomplished things and never received any acknowledgments. He painfully recognizes that feeling worthless is one of his key repressed fears.

Now it makes sense to Henry why he's clashed with his boss, former girlfriend, and even one of his close friends. Since they did not provide the recognition he desperately needed to feel loved and valued, he reacted emotionally and pushed them away. Through this personal work, he suddenly experiences an insightful epiphany! All those people were playing their part in his destructive drama cycles to make him understand his vulnerability.

With this insightful self-knowledge and a deep understanding of his subconscious programming, Henry is set up for success as he prepares to question his next trigger. He no longer feels that others are the problem. As a matter of fact, he feels confident the key to happiness is in his own hands if he can process the repressed fears of worthlessness.

Sure enough, the next trigger happens. His boss criticizes him for not getting something done in time, even though he knows Henry had a few time-consuming projects that created schedule conflicts. Instead of his usual angry lashing out, Henry pauses and observes his thoughts. He then realizes, having done the reverse engineering work, *Oh, wait a second, I'm angry because I feel my boss is not seeing my worth. I feel put down and unappreciated as they ignore my diligent efforts to finish those projects on time.*

How can you achieve this kind of introspection during a trigger event? When you continue your Daily Review practice, you slowly develop the skill to connect the dots between your emotions, thoughts, feelings, and repressed fears more quickly and naturally within moments. Over time, the deeper understanding and insights you gain from triggers give you more opportunities to pause and observe for more profound insights.

What if I can't access such a deep understanding of my past? What else can I do to review my childhood experiences to identify my repressed fears?

You may experience some difficulty in correlating your current feelings to your past. It's completely normal to find it challenging to delve into past experiences and untangle the complex repressed fears tied to the current situations you experience. You may struggle to understand how your parents or other adults may have affected your subconscious programming that controls your emotional reactions today.

I shared a list of questions below to help you gather information about your childhood. Review them thoroughly. To answer them, you need people. Can you reach out to your parents? How about talking to some of your relatives? Are you in touch with your friends from college, high school, or elementary school? Maybe they could shed some light on these questions.

Conversations with different people who knew you from your past, along with the questions below, may guide you to deeper realizations, revealing profound and intriguing insights on why you emotionally react to people and how your past has formed your repressed fears that ultimately govern your life today.

- How did your parents treat you growing up?
- How was the relationship between your parents?
- What is their life story? How did your parents grow up? How was their relationship with their parents? (Most of our repressed fears are ancestral patterns passed from our parents on to us. So, learning about your parents and their lives may provide valuable information about how they treated you and how your repressed fears were formed.)
- What was your dynamic with your siblings and your parents' attitude toward you and them? Pay attention to the age difference. Ask your parents how a new sibling affected you at the time. Or, if you are the younger one, inquire how it was growing up behind your siblings. If you are the middle child, investigate how you managed the relationships between siblings and how well or poorly your parents related to you and them.
- Was one or both of your parents not emotionally available to you? If so, what impacted your social behavior and relationships with your friends?
- Was one or both of your parents physically absent growing up? How did you cope with their absence?
- Was one or both of your parents controlling and disciplinary? What characteristics and personality have

you adopted to deal with such strict treatment? Did you become rebellious or conformist?

- Was one or both of your parents demanding and approving? What part of you wanted to please them? Have you become sensitive to others' needs, beginning with seeking your parents' approval?
- What was your parents' primary expectation of you? How did you respond to this expectation?
- How did your parents' divorce, if applicable, affect you? Or, if they're still together, how did their fights and arguments make you feel? Did you think it was your fault that they were not happy? Did you want to save their marriage? Do you avoid conflicts?

The list is helpful. At the same time, while reviewing these questions, I couldn't help but reflect on how much my parents and their actions have influenced my repressed fears and the way I live my life today. Does everyone blame their parents for having these unprocessed feelings?

As I mentioned earlier in the introduction, no relationship is perfect at its core. As a whole, parents struggle to live consciously, often bound by their own repressed fears that their parents most likely passed onto them.

The solution is to become more aware of who we are and why we emotionally react to each other. My grandma often asked my dad why he was so angry with us, his children. But he did not have a good answer. In the end, though, such anger caused a tremendous amount of not good enough in my sister and me. My dad didn't wake up every morning intending to hurt us; however, his complete lack of awareness forced him to act and react subconsciously, resulting in tremendous emotional pain for his children.

You can blame your parents for their wrongdoings, but your attention on them will not help you process your underlying repressed fears. Today, your own subconscious fight-or-flight defense mechanisms are at work in your home with your family. What remains unprocessed in your subconscious affects your children in much the same way your parents' unresolved past affected you. Without intending, you may end up causing your children to develop their own repressed fears.

Not surprisingly, these fears are usually very similar to yours. In a way, it's one of life's mischievous jokes on us. Since you couldn't process your repressed fears before parenthood, you pass them on through emotional reactions to your children. Such reactions come from the projection of your own unprocessed fears. Ironically, you are now faced with the same issues daily. If you avoid your personal growth, the responsibility of processing such fears passes on to your children.

The solution or path to happiness is not blaming your parents but understanding their role in your repressed fears. They, like you, experienced hurtful events as a child, and no one taught them how to cope with these intense feelings. Even today, as adults, most of us don't have the tools to process those repressed fears properly. Fortunately, you can start making changes now and profoundly affect future generations.

Once you begin your personal work and reverse engineer your thoughts to decipher your subconscious programming, you can break the cycle of passing on repressed fears from one generation to another. Learning emotional mastery skills will not only improve your own life but also positively impact the lives of your spouse, children, and everybody else you interact with regularly.

I didn't think processing my repressed fears could have so much influence on my surroundings as well as on my ancestral line. I want to understand them and learn about them. Do you have a list of common repressed fears I can use during my Daily Review?

Certainly. Here is a list of the most common repressed fears and a few possible origins of each.

> **Fear of Not Being Good Enough:** Strict, judgmental, or controlling parents who closely monitored every activity and gave negative feedback or constant instructions on how to do things "right."
>
> **Fear of Not Being Recognized:** Distant, aloof, emotionally unavailable parents who ignored you and your accomplishments and who provided little or no feedback.
>
> **Fear of Loneliness:** Oblivious, dismissive parents who didn't acknowledge your existence and didn't interact with you, either on an intimate or a day-to-day level.
>
> **Fear of Abandonment:** Being left behind by parents due to unexpected circumstances; one day, everything fell apart, leaving you on your own and making you lose trust in people and life.
>
> **Fear of Failure:** Parents who constantly encourage your activities but give and share love on the condition of achieving success and good results.
>
> **Fear of Betrayal:** Parents who compared you to your friends and took their side while measuring you against their behavior and performance; instances where you felt you were cheated on in a relationship.

Fear of Not Being Valued: Parents who ignored you or were emotionally unavailable without acknowledgment of what you did for them; being the middle child, stuck between high-achieving older siblings and attention-seeking younger siblings.

Fear of Rejection: Controlling, unacknowledging parents who gave you almost no time and space for your personality to develop, made decisions on your behalf, and gave no feedback to nurture your development.

Fear of Success, Impostor Syndrome: Encouraging, hard-working parents who sacrificed to give you opportunities to succeed, but with a lot of pressure to climb to the top.

Fear of Missing Out: Lazy or argumentative parents who had daily routines and tasks to be followed without spontaneity, excitement, or fun.

Fear of Not Being Approved Of: Highly disciplinary, self-centered parents with detail-oriented personalities who controlled everything with the idea that there's only one right answer or solution.

Fear of Financial Instability: Experiencing sudden financial loss growing up, parents who declared bankruptcy, or parents or ancestors who moved to a new country and started with almost nothing.

Now take a brief moment. Do any of the above repressed fears resonate with you?

You don't have to immediately identify with a repressed fear. You can wait until the next trigger event. When experiencing one, you can pause and observe your thoughts to access your subconscious programming on full display. Then, you can simply run another reverse engineering process by diving deep into your repressed fears that may have caused your emotional reactions.

What do I do after I discover what my repressed fears are?

When you relentlessly perform reverse engineering to almost every trigger event, you see a cluster of feelings that appear frequently. These feelings are common themes that run your entire life. They are woven into every interaction. They lie dormant underneath every relationship until seemingly unrelated triggers provoke them and activate the repressed fears you've been carrying since your childhood.

When you train yourself to slow down your emotional reactions during those trigger events, you now have a few more seconds to bring this incredibly valuable self-knowledge forward into your consciousness, as well as in your interactions to ward off the provokers of your repressed fears and reclaim your boundaries against the people who crossed them.

You can accomplish this goal by using I-Feel Statements, which is your second Communication Strategy. After all, you have been running away from the people who provoke your repressed fears and expose your vulnerability all your life. The time has come to face those people head-on and confront their challenges directly and openly, regardless of how painful and difficult it will be.

Facing your repressed fears and revealing them to others honestly and assertively also helps you deeply process them. Whatever is in the dark needs to come to light. Whatever is repressed needs to be expressed. Why? Because what we carry as emotional baggage in the body makes life heavy. By expressing them freely, we release the burden of the past.

SECOND COMMUNICATION STRATEGY: USING I-FEEL STATEMENTS

I-Feel Statements are basically reflections of your repressed fears in the form of intimate feelings that, in the past, you haven't dared to share with anybody because you didn't know about them. How could you? It's nobody's fault, but you didn't know how to be aware of them, understand them, and eventually process them. I-Feel Statements help you bring your attention back to yourself and your feelings. Yes, others make you feel in a certain way, but how will you respond to them? You now know the only way to process your repressed fears is to express your feelings exactly in the moment when you're triggered.

When using I-Feel Statements, it's important to know that your feelings are yours and are absolutely non-negotiable. They are your proprietary information and have nothing to do with anyone else, even though others may play their part to trigger them. Therefore, do not expect anything from others when you express your feelings. These I-Feel Statements are for you to reveal something intimate, special, and vulnerable that your subconscious has hidden away your entire life.

Use I-Feel Statements with the utmost sincerity and honesty, without any intention of manipulation. Simply share your feelings as facts. Just focus on what's really going on within you. That's all. No one can argue with you and force you to feel a certain way. When you use I-Feel Statements to share your feelings and experiences without assigning blame, you stay in your own lane, not putting others on defense.

For example, when someone doesn't acknowledge what you did for them and makes you feel unappreciated, you can say, "I felt unappreciated when I didn't hear any feedback on what I did." In another example, when someone changes their plans and doesn't communicate it to you, you can share, "I felt ignored and not valued when I was not informed about the last-minute changes in our plans."

When you reflect on your inner world like this and state what's going on inside of you, I-Feel Statements can be great tools for establishing healthy boundaries in all relationships. After all, power doesn't lie in how well you can hide your repressed fears but in how courageously you can own and express them to yourself and others. This second Communication Strategy requires much more awareness on your part, so it will challenge you more than Doing the Opposite.

What if others get offended when I use I-Feel Statements?

You may offend others if your strategy includes the following:

1. You-Statements

Most of us make the mistake of adding a condition when using I-Feel Statements. For example, when your partner doesn't listen to you when you talk or rarely interacts with you because they're on their cell phones all the time, you may say, "I feel ignored and unseen because you never pay attention to me! You're always occupied with other things and never spend quality time with me." This is not an I-Feel Statement but an accusation. By using "you," you're blaming them for making you feel unseen. Why? Because your feelings are tied to a condition, and you want them to change. That desire for them to alter their behavior so that you feel happy comes from your defensive thoughts.

Even though it's your reality—which reflects your own truth—it may not be the other person's reality.

When you accuse them of hurting you, they will immediately get defensive. As a result, they will start explaining themselves and offer excuses for why that particular situation happened.

As we discussed earlier, every defense becomes an offense. When the other person takes your conditioned statements or accusations personally, they come back with their own version of that condition. Of course, you won't accept their explanation because whatever they say will sound like you're not seen, heard, respected, and so on. And as you can appreciate, such arguments go on forever, and now you know why.

To avoid these endless exchanges, try using I-Feel Statements like a monologue and only talk about your own feelings. After all, expressing your vulnerability is a sign of strength, not a weakness. Broadcast your feelings, impressions, thoughts, perceptions, and even emotions, and describe exactly what's happening inside you without making any reference to the other person.

For example, when your partner ignores your latest accomplishment at work or misses your birthday every year, you can deploy an I-Feel Statement with a longer monologue, "I'm angry. I feel ignored and unrecognized. I received more good news at work and feel I can't celebrate fully. It's frustrating to me when I can't share such moments with my partner. I'm also sad. My birthday is important to me. I'm curious why we can't turn these days into special occasions and celebrate together."

This openness, although it's vulnerable, will break the ice with your partner who just triggered you and smooth the tense, feisty energy by bringing you two closer through a more sincere and honest dialogue.

2. Emotion-Statements

Another big mistake we often make when using I-Feel Statements is mixing up our emotions with our feelings. Statements such as "I feel angry" or "I feel frustrated" are not I-Feel Statements. Those are emotions and don't belong in I-Feel Statements. You can say, "I am angry because I feel ignored," but using an emotion statement alone doesn't give the other person enough information about your state of mind.

Since emotions carry the charge of your repressed fears, simply stating them may confuse or even offend others. You may unintentionally force them to defend their position. For example, when someone's comments make you angry, and you say, "I feel angry," the other person may immediately question your emotion and throw in a few defensive explanations: "Why are you angry? I didn't mean to say that. You're making a big deal out of it. You are so sensitive."

Now, imagine, instead, you say, "I am angry because I feel put down and criticized." They may still question why you feel the way you do, but then, you can acknowledge that, regardless of their intent, you still feel put down and criticized. Do you see how easily you can stand by your feelings when they're not negotiable? They're simply yours to own. On the contrary, stating your emotions opens up the conversation to debate, which could lead to endless arguments because your emotions stem from your defensive thoughts. I hope the difference between I-Feel Statements and emotion-statements is clear. Try both, and notice the difference.

3. Explanation-Statements

Explanations are justifications of why you feel a certain way. For example, when your best friend doesn't text you back for a few days or, on another occasion, supports another friend's opinion over yours, you might end up feeling abandoned. That's okay. It's only natural. But how are you going to communicate your feelings to your friend? You might say, "When I didn't hear back from you, I felt abandoned because I want to be best friends with you, and I don't appreciate you not texting me for a few days, as I feel lonely and betrayed because I trust you to be my bestie. I'm sensitive to these things because my parents got divorced when I was five years old. I can't deal with this kind of behavior."

I-Feel Statements carry almost the opposite energy of explanations or justifications. You don't need to defend your feelings; they're factual and don't require outside evaluation or validation. Therefore, you don't need to prepare a doctoral dissertation when sharing your feelings with others. Instead, make your I-Feel Statements short and precise. "I feel abandoned." (Period!) "I feel betrayed. And I feel lonely and disconnected." (Period!)

You don't have to explain, justify, or defend them further. Explaining yourself pushes you into a defensive stance and compromises your boundaries. The other person may immediately pick up on that and start arguing with you by challenging your explanations, even your feelings.

When emotionally charged, you may be tempted to explain yourself. However, if you do, you won't get what you want out of the conversation. The dialogue will quickly become a "you said, I said" pattern. When you still feel the need to explain and don't have the right energy to be factual, neutral, and matter-of-fact, practice I-Feel Statements on your own. Simply share your emotions, thoughts, feelings, and whatever else is surfacing in your Daily Review to yourself. Write them all out in your Daily Review Journal. By getting them off your chest, you can process them, potentially lessening the need to express them during future trigger events.

How do I respond when the other person accuses me of being too sensitive?

When someone doesn't accept your I-Feel Statement and tries to dismiss your feelings by labeling you as "too sensitive," you can always anchor your energy and mindset in facts. Your feelings are non-negotiable. They belong to you. You have them and don't need to justify or defend them. No one can argue with you about why you're having them. If they were in your shoes and had experienced the same past situations, they might have similar repressed fears and vulnerabilities.

In addition to being too sensitive, you may also hear judgments that you're thin-skinned and make a big deal out of nothing. Others may say you shouldn't feel that way. They may switch tactics and try to intimidate you. In these cases, they don't usually make these statements out of ill will or bad intentions but because they feel defensive, uncomfortable, or guilty that they made you feel that way.

They simply want to fix how you're feeling and avoid conflict, discomfort, and hurt. That's their defensive agenda. Not yours. Every offense is defensive. If they're verbally attacking you, that means something makes them uncomfortable and defensive.

No matter what the situation is, do not ignore your feelings.

Own them. Acknowledge your sensitivity. Your answer to them may be a simple yes: "Yes, that's how I feel. And yes, I am sensitive. My feelings are not negotiable."

That feels scary. Why would I make myself so vulnerable?

You have been hiding your vulnerability behind your defensive actions. What has changed in your life when you've defended yourself against triggers with intense emotional reactions over the years? Nothing. You still experience triggers. With the first Communication Strategy, you started to respond differently, and because of that, you deserve to expect different outcomes. The second Communication Strategy encourages you to face your vulnerability with I-Feel Statements and change the energy of fruitless arguments into thoughtful dialogues.

Facing vulnerability helps you process your repressed fears by no longer hiding them or running away from them. As their intensity decreases, you react less to people's comments and attitudes. Practicing these Communication Strategies builds a foundation for emotional mastery.

Putting yourself out there and sharing your feelings with others in open and sincere dialogue will be awkward at first, but this is an opportunity for you to adjust how you interact with others and clear the heavy weight of the past. I-Feel Statements are great strategies to rewrite your past by empowering you to express your authentic feelings. Some describe this transformation as a "coming out" party or a rebirth, as you begin a new chapter by standing up for yourself and asserting your boundaries.

Can you share some more examples to make the first two steps of the Power Method and their respective Communication Strategies clearer?

In a nutshell, emotional mastery brings happiness, deeper connections, and more meaningful relationships into your life. By growing personally and processing your repressed fears, you free yourself from your past trauma and childhood emotional baggage.

Here are some life-real scenarios you can reflect on to get a sense of what kind of positive shift you can create in your life.

Scenario One

The Trigger: Jennifer is super excited that the weather will be amazing this weekend, so she has planned a road trip with her family to the beach. She's anticipating a lovely day with her husband, Mike, and the kids. However, as they hit the road, they realize everyone in town had the same idea, so the road is jam-packed with other cars. Jennifer, with her upbeat and positive personality, starts playing music on Spotify to keep the energy happy and light. Suddenly, she hears her husband yelling and cursing at the car trying to cut in front of them into their lane. Jennifer knew he frequently displayed road rage, but this time, she thinks his impatience is uncalled for. Traffic is deadlocked, and they aren't going anywhere fast. So, what is this all about? As she looks at him, her husband continues to display his anger and makes rude hand and finger gestures at the other driver who is straddling the two lanes because Jennifer's husband won't give them enough space to fully pull into their lane. Jennifer sits quietly, steaming inside, and then notices the kids' horrified expressions in the back seat.

Emotions: Jennifer experiences anger, frustration, anxiety, and embarrassment almost simultaneously.

Thoughts: She worries about the potential for conflict and feels angry with her husband because she thinks he's being rude, arrogant, disrespectful, and inconsiderate. She's frustrated because she thinks her husband does this all the time. It is another potentially great day that has been ruined by his temper. She's anxious because she thinks her kids are negatively impacted and worries about what kind of psychological effects this will have on them. And finally, Jennifer is embarrassed because she believes everybody should respect each other and get along without conflicts, and her husband is violating her values on all accounts.

Feelings: Jennifer feels devalued, invisible, disrespected, and out of sorts.

Repressed Fears: Fear of getting into conflict, fear of being hurt, fear of not being valued, fear of disconnection, and fear of being invisible.

Origins: During her Daily Review, Jennifer recalls how she witnessed her dad have similar outbursts growing up, with such a short fuse at the dinner table almost every night. No matter how carefully Jennifer, her sister, and her mom behaved, her dad could always find something to be angry about. She observed how her mom stayed quiet to avoid escalating the situation. Meanwhile, Jennifer would try to cheer her dad up with some positive remarks to make the conflict go away. Because she watched her parents disconnect from each other, Jennifer subconsciously decided to always be cheerful and warm and tried to avoid drama at all costs.

Old Reactions: Before practicing emotional mastery training, Jennifer avoided confrontations like her mom did. So, it was difficult to override her subconscious programming and say anything during these conflicts with her husband. Usually, he was the one who started the fight while she avoided confrontation, trying to keep the peace for the family's sake.

New Response: After digging into her programming and the patterns it created, Jennifer realizes that nothing will change unless she changes how she handles these situations. She remembers Doing the Opposite and I-Feel Statements as possible strategies. So, she decides to speak up in front of her kids while her husband exchanges words with the other driver. She collects her courage, as this is the first time she has intentionally engaged with the conflict rather than running away from it, and says, "Hey Mike, what's going on? I'm angry right now and feel we're ruining our day. Having one more car in front of us when we have a hundred others not going anywhere is not that important. I don't want to be stuck in traffic for hours, either! What choice do we have? Yet, you're not making it easier to bear it. If you don't want to go to the beach in this traffic, let's turn around at the next exit."

Her husband gets quiet, rolls up the window, and looks at Jennifer as if he's seeing her for the first time. He is visibly embarrassed, like a kid caught trying to steal candy from the jar next to the cashier at the grocery store. He takes a deep breath in, takes his time exhaling, and says, "I know of a great café in the next town. Why don't we stop there, have something to eat, and then decide if we still want to go to the beach? Maybe traffic will open up by then." And he winks to Jennifer, who, surprisingly, realizes she has a few tears in her eyes as she recognizes the fun-loving, positive, and resourceful man she married.

Scenario Two

The Trigger: Tom complains that no matter how hard he works, his boss never appreciates his efforts. The day before the monthly executive meeting that his boss attends and wants Tom to prepare the slides for, they are both sitting in a conference room, reviewing the material Tom has prepared over the last couple of days. The meeting kicks off with his boss making a nitpicky comment about the subpoints under each heading not being indented enough on the first slide. Tom is taken aback by the comment, but because these monthly executive meetings are so important for his boss to showcase his talent, Tom lets it slide. As they continue going through the slides, his boss gets visibly irritated—not about the content, but by how Tom chose to present it. At one point, his boss starts to raise his voice. As Tom begins to explain his reasoning, his boss gets up, takes his computer, and leaves the conference room. Tom sits there, shaken, disturbed, and shocked.

Emotions: Tom experiences overwhelming anger at being so disrespectfully left behind in the conference room. He also feels resentful about working for a boss with such low emotional intelligence.

Thoughts: Tom thinks his boss is out to get him. In Tom's opinion, his boss doesn't treat him like the other employees. Tom also thinks his boss is arrogant but doesn't know what he's doing. Tom questions why he is still working at this company despite his boss's attitude toward him.

Feelings: Tom feels devalued, unseen, poorly regarded, disrespected, and unrecognized for his efforts.

Repressed Fears: Fear of not being recognized and valued.

Origins: After further reflection during his Daily Review, Tom realizes that his dad never recognized how much Tom wanted to connect with him. Tom participated in sports to get his dad's attention and spend time with him. However, his dad always found a way to criticize him. Whether it was homework, how he threw the basketball, interacted with his friends, or behaved at home, his dad always found something to pick on. It dawns on Tom that he's always felt the need to cater to authority figures to meet this instinctive urge to be recognized.

Old Reaction: Usually, when things get to this level of confrontation and disconnect, Tom starts to look for another job. This has happened a few times before, and every time, he lands a new position within a month or two. This process always makes Tom feel good that others recognize his value. He's already thinking about updating his résumé and reaching out to a couple of recruiters he worked with.

New Response: After reflecting on his last few jobs and how he reacted to people there, Tom realizes he has an opportunity for change. In other words, he's attracted a trigger prompting him to work on his repressed fears. Because of this revelation, he decides to try Doing the Opposite and share his I-Feel Statements with his boss. He stops updating his résumé. He wants to fight for his current job and not give his power away.

The next day, Tom sets up a one-on-one meeting with his boss in a different conference room from their usual one. When they sit down, Tom gets right into it by nervously saying, "I don't understand what happened yesterday. I feel confused about what was so bad in the presentation that you felt you had to leave the room. Recently, I've been feeling unappreciated for the work I'm doing for you. I put in a lot of effort to make you look good, but you say that my work always comes up short. I feel unrecognized and unvalued when I only get reactions and no feedback."

Tom's boss listens attentively and tries to make sense of what Tom is getting at. He doesn't quite understand what the problem is. He stays quiet. He nods to show that he's hearing Tom. But soon after, he stands up and says, "Thanks for sharing all of this. I'll try to work with you more closely in the future. All good now?" Whether Tom's boss will ultimately change his attitude or not is not that important. What matters is that Tom voiced his frustration and discontent and shared his I-Feel Statements. Once he expressed that, Tom felt much more relaxed and lighter, and he didn't push himself as hard to get his boss's attention because he realized that he was projecting his craving for his dad's recognition onto his boss.

Scenario Three

The trigger: Emily is excited about her weekend plans to meet with her friend June and see a new Oscar-nominated movie. The forecast is for cold, rainy weather—perfect for seeing a film and then going out to a café for coffee and discussion afterward—and she is looking forward to the outing. However, Emily is also a little worried because June doesn't have a good concept of time, and Emily hates missing the opening of movies. She especially doesn't want to miss the beginning of this one because it's been so well-reviewed. Sure enough, Emily finds herself waiting in the cold in front of the movie theater. She checks her phone for messages. None. Now, only a few more minutes before the movie starts, Emily remembers how deliberately she'd warned her friend not to be late.

Emotions: Emily is furious. She knew this was going to happen. She's angry, disappointed, and extremely frustrated.

Thoughts: Emily thinks her friend is simply oblivious to everyone else's preferences. She believes her friend is completely disrespecting her. She questions their friendship: "How dare she not care for me and let me wait in the cold for her? What kind of a friend is she?"

Feelings: Emily feels disrespected, disregarded, unimportant, and like nobody. She also feels lonely. Who else is there to socialize with? She realizes she doesn't have many friends she feels close with.

Repressed Fears: Fear of not having someone you can trust, fear of being disregarded, fear of not being important, fear of being lonely.

Origins: Emily reflects on her repressed fears and time travels to her childhood. She acknowledges that she is the youngest of four siblings and how it has affected her psyche. Because of the age difference between the siblings (she was five years younger than the youngest of the other siblings), the others always did things together and didn't take Emily with them. Emily always had a sense that she was being left behind. Suddenly, Emily accesses her subconscious programming and has the deeper realization that she believes no one will treat her as if she's important since her own siblings didn't. As a result, she has lost trust in people.

Old Reaction: This realization makes Emily understand that her old reaction of getting angry comes from testing people to see if she can trust them. She gives them opportunities to come through for her, and of course, because it's her limiting life pattern, she never feels that anyone really does. Then, she gets angry at them for failing to meet her expectations. But because she doesn't want to lose them, like she didn't want to lose her siblings, she continues to live with her disappointment without being rude to her friends.

New Response: After realizing her subconscious programming and how not trusting people created her limiting life patterns, Emily decides to use this opportunity to change things up. She immediately activates the Doing the Opposite strategy. She texts her friend about three minutes before the movie starts and tells her she's going in to catch the beginning. She leaves June's ticket at the ticket box office, goes in, and takes her seat right before the movie is about to start. She thinks to herself, *if my friend takes offense and gets upset with me, it's her problem.*

June shows up fifteen minutes late, apologizing profusely. Emily shushes her and gives her a fake smile. After the movie, they head to the café. Emily, still stewing with anger and frustration, decides to use her I-Feel Statements. She says, "You know how much I hate being late to movies or even to any meetings, period. I mentioned to you that this movie was important to me, and I felt disrespected that we didn't meet on time." She then decides to share a bit more personal information on how difficult it is to trust her friends due to her sibling relationship.

June is visibly sad and apologizes for her lateness, explaining that she'd lost her car key and then found it in her jacket pocket but had to rush to get to the movie theater, so she didn't have time to text Emily. She affirms her deep care for Emily and how much she values the friendship. With that, Emily's friend never shows up late to their meetings again, but Emily also isn't as worried as she was before because she has released her repressed fears of mistrust and not being important.

JOURNAL ENTRY FOR WEEK TWO

For the next seven days, make a journal entry at the end of each day to capture the most intense trigger event that occurred. Do this review by answering the following questions:

1. What was the trigger event?
2. What emotions did you experience?
3. What thoughts did you have?
4. What were your feelings?
5. Can you identify your repressed fears?
6. What are their origins?
7. What is your typical reaction?
8. What will be your new Communication Strategy?

DAILY CHECKLIST FOR WEEK TWO

1. Have you practiced the following Power Steps?

   - Pause to notice your emotions
   - Observe your thoughts

2. Have you practiced the following Power Techniques?

   - Square Breathing
   - Self-Observation Meditation

3. Have you practiced the following Power Tools?

   - I'm {the emotion}
   - What If—So What

4. Have you used any of the following Communication Strategies?

   - Doing the Opposite
   - Using I-Feel Statements

CHAPTER FOUR

GOING BEYOND THE MIND

Processing Trauma through the Body

Imagine sitting in traffic, seemingly relaxed, when suddenly a song on the radio instantly tightens your chest and brings tears to your eyes. You're surprised by the physical reaction, yet the heaviness and sadness feel all too familiar. It's as if this music and its lyrics activate a hidden part of yourself, pulling you back to an emotional state from the past you thought you'd already processed a long time ago.

Have you ever experienced something similar, where your body acts on its own, responding with anger, frustration, and anxiety without having control over these emotions? Through the work you've done so far, you now know that these emotions come from your thoughts and feelings that resulted in past trauma.

The I-Feel Statements that you started using will help you decouple your thoughts from your feelings. But that's only at the mental level. The repressed fears, which are the root cause of your emotional reactions, are not only in your mind, but they're in your body, too. Therefore, to process your past trauma and decondition your subconscious programming, you need to get your body involved.

What if you could connect with those physical sensations you experience during trigger events? What if they were the signposts of where the subconscious has stored repressed fears? What if you could acknowledge them during those intense emotional reactions and understand their origins? What if, through this deeper work, you could release them for good?

Imagine the freedom and lightness from letting go of years of repressed emotional wounds. In this chapter, we'll explore how the third Power Step, Welcome, helps you connect with your body and process and heal what's held within.

This kind of somatic healing takes place in the body yet profoundly affects the mental and emotional states of your being. When you welcome your physical sensations—in other words, acknowledge them, no matter how painful they are—you allow your body to integrate all parts of yourself.

Through this integration, you honor the signals in your body and learn to process them thoroughly for greater presence and emotional mastery. You're about to expand your journey toward healing your past trauma that goes beyond the mind, tapping into the deep wisdom of your emotions trapped in your body.

Can you tell me more about why I need mental, emotional, and physical healing?

Because what is really being repressed during a traumatic event has mental, emotional, and physical components. When we experience the original trigger event, we feel intimidated. We feel threatened. Our safety is in jeopardy. That's why we think we don't have the power to state our thoughts (mental), express our feelings (emotional), and take a stance to set healthy boundaries (physical). We feel forced to suppress them all. We feel "victimized"—rightfully and naturally! In that state, we feel powerless to do anything. In a sense, the Power Method is designed to help everyone regain their power and no longer fear those who victimized them.

On the mental side, we internalize the way others make us feel. We start to believe that we're not good enough to be liked, not worthy enough to be recognized, not useful enough to be valued, and so on. These subconscious thought patterns and belief systems lie dormant in the mental part of our being until we're triggered.

On the emotional side, we repress our feelings of not being good enough, not being recognized, not being valued, and so on, along with our emotions of anger, sadness, anxiety, resentment, and so on. These feelings and emotions remain unprocessed in the emotional part of our being until they come to the surface when we face a challenging situation.

And finally, on the physical side, we repress the physical sensations that we experience during those traumatic events. Most of us don't feel these sensations because we get "out of the body" to avoid feeling pain—not just emotional or mental but also physical pain—during such emotionally wounding events. We simply shut our bodies down and refuse to acknowledge physical sensations because they are too painful to handle. These unprocessed physical sensations are stored in the body and may be the source of physical illness we experience later in life.

Practicing the 5-Step Power Method helps you process and heal your past trauma on these three layers of your being. The first two steps, Pause and Observe, address what's being repressed on the mental and emotional planes, while the third Power Step, Welcome, empowers you to deal with the emotionally traumatic events trapped in your body.

Interesting. How do I welcome the physical sensations in a way that will help me process the repressed fears stored in my body?

You've been working on being present in the very instance you're triggered. That moment carries so much information about you, your subconscious, and your past trauma. Therefore, you need to get in touch with the physical sensations that your emotions create in your body as another resource to accumulate more data about your repressed fears.

Always remember and pay attention to the fact that every emotion you experience has a corresponding physical sensation in the body. The locations of such emotional charges indicate where your body holds your repressed fears. When you welcome these painful sensations, you also get out of your head and out of your thoughts and drop into your body, making it easier to process what's being repressed in that spot.

Here's your third Power Technique, 3-by-3 Breath, to help you execute the third Power Step, Welcome.

THIRD POWER TECHNIQUE: 3-BY-3 BREATH

In this technique, you use your breath to release the tense energy stuck in your body, where repressed fears have been held for years. With regular practice of the 3-by-3 Breath technique, you'll be surprised by how much less personally you take triggers and how the intensity of the emotional reactions gradually decreases over time.

Apply this third Power Technique whenever you feel an emotional charge in your body. Of course, this naturally happens when you're triggered. Right there and then, you first pause and observe, and then inhale deeply into the physical sensation of the emotional charge and hold your breath for three seconds. While holding, keep your focus on the physical sensation and nothing else. Next, exhale to release the charge, the sensations, and the associated repressed fears out of your mouth. Just imagine you're coughing them out of your body with moderate force. Practice this breath routine three times in a row. Hence, the name 3-by-3 Breath: three cycles of inhale and exhale with a three-second hold in between.

As you can imagine, when inhaling into painful physical sensations, you basically face the pain and the repressed fears associated with them. Every time you apply this technique, you slowly take out small chunks of your fears and process them by releasing them from your body. Experiment with it. Every time you exhale, you feel lighter as you consciously let go of the heaviness of past trauma. This lightness eventually translates into softer and lower-intensity physical sensations.

Shall I apply the 3-by-3 Breath in the middle of a trigger event or after, when I'm reviewing the situation during my Daily Review?

Well, you can do both. Yes, there are two applications of the 3-by-3 Breath. The first is a longer process, where you apply the Power Method to a trigger event during your Daily Review after the fact by remembering it in the comfort of your home. You can do this at the end of the day simply by reflecting on the trigger event and reliving it while observing yourself from the outside to note all the subtle emotions, thoughts, feelings, repressed fears, and physical sensations you experienced. And while you're feeling all that in your body, you can apply the 3-by-3 Breath to release the emotional charge, physical sensations, and associated repressed fears.

The second application is during a trigger event in the heat of the moment.

However, in the beginning, it may be difficult to locate the physical sensations in your body. This difficulty comes from the fact that triggers hook into the mental and emotional parts of your being and block your ability to expand your awareness of your body. As a result, whenever you launch your fight-or-flight defense mechanisms, you're stuck trying to defend yourself against triggers mentally and emotionally, and you end up ceding complete control to your subconscious programming, which prevents you from dropping into the body.

Slowing down your emotional reactions with Pause and Observe and bringing your attention inward opens up the possibility of getting more awareness into your body. You simply start to sense physical sensations, such as tension, tightness, contraction, and heaviness, that result from your emotional reactions to triggers.

Then, your third Power Step, Welcome, is all about acknowledging and accepting—in other words, welcoming—what arises in your body as physical sensations resulting from a trigger event. As we discussed earlier, these physical sensations indicate where your repressed fears are stored in the body when the original traumatic events take place. By locating and processing them through the 3-by-3 Breath, you start healing past wounds in the physical part of your being.

This third Power Step can be somewhat difficult because you are about to face the emotional pain that you've been trying to avoid your entire life. Therefore, you may experience a natural internal resistance. To break this resistance, you may want to lean into this discomfort and break the subconscious programming so that it feels safe to release control over its fight-or-flight defense mechanisms. Once this release occurs, you can execute the 3-by-3 Breath flawlessly and process as much of your repressed fear as possible in one breath.

If you do experience unwillingness to go into the discomfort, that is very natural and understandable. After all, you're about to open old wounds and experience the associated painful memories. However, it's vital to have a deep awareness of your physical sensations. That's why we have a practice called Conscious Discomfort, which is your next tool.

THIRD POWER TOOL: CONSCIOUS DISCOMFORT

Conscious Discomfort means that you simply sit with painful physical sensations and consciously experience the discomfort, tension, contraction, heaviness, tightness, or whatever else you may be feeling in your body at the time of a trigger or when reviewing a trigger event during your Daily Review practice. In this practice, you have to immerse yourself fully in the discomfort. Just like in the Self-Observation Meditation, you only need to observe the pain and the physical sensations for a few seconds during the heat of the moment or for a few minutes during your review of your daily emotional reactions.

The reasoning behind the Conscious Discomfort technique is the same as the Doing the Opposite strategy. You're going to use the same approach to processing your repressed fears. Remember, when you felt emotional discomfort the first time, it was so painful that you repressed it, and your subconscious programming was formed to protect it. Now, you're going to do the opposite. Instead of hiding from it, you're going to face it. Doing this sends your subconscious a message that you feel safer now and no longer need its protection. You are now ready to stand up and are no longer intimidated by trigger events that threaten to expose your vulnerability and repressed fears and inflict emotional pain.

Since trigger events exist in your life because you have related repressed fears, isn't it interesting to think that life is on your side and wants you to lighten the burden of emotional wounds that you have been carrying for decades? To help you with that, life subtly brings you these trigger events to point you in the right direction. Where? Back to your body and toward your repressed fears so you can process and release them once and for all.

The only reason you have triggers in your life is because you have repressed fears. They're the messengers for your vulnerability.

From that perspective, they provide a great opportunity for processing. However, if you defend yourself against triggers, you look outward, in the wrong direction, away from your personal growth.

Instead, suppose you turn inward and allow yourself to process your past trauma. In that case, you feel lighter, your awareness expands, your understanding of yourself and your life deepens, and slowly but surely, you start to have all sorts of new experiences where you can embrace a drama-free, joyful, and fulfilling life.

It's challenging to stay in the discomfort. How can I use the 3-by-3 Breath effectively to practice Conscious Discomfort?

Let's tackle your question with an example. My client, Kathy, loses her inspiration and motivation to work on an important project she is supposed to finish over the weekend. It's so important that getting her next promotion is dependent on finishing it. But even though she knows this is a highly visible project and needs to get it done, she can't focus and finds herself wasting a lot of time watching TV, scrolling on social media, and surfing the internet instead of allocating time to her work.

It's in one of these moments that she realizes her project is triggering her, and that's why she procrastinates. So, she employs the 5-Step Power Method to get to the root of what's bothering her.

First, she immediately pauses to notice her emotions: *Frustration.*

Then, she asks herself why she is frustrated: *I'm not spending time on what's urgent and important; instead, I'm wasting time on stupid stuff.*

She then observes her thoughts: *Oh, no, I'm procrastinating and wasting time! There goes my promotion!*

Right after she observes her thoughts, she launches the reverse engineering process and starts asking "What If—So What" Questions to challenge her thoughts:

What if I don't get the promotion I want so what? How would that make me feel?

I'll be embarrassed in front of my boss, colleagues, family, and friends.

What if I'm embarrassed in front of my boss, colleagues, family, and friends? So what? How would that make me feel?

I'll look like an idiot, like I don't know what I'm doing, and potentially lose momentum in my career.

What if I fall behind in my career? So what? How would that make me feel?

I'll be a total failure and feel like a loser.

She feels comfortable with how deep she goes with the "What If—So What" Questions, so she questions whether this feeling of failure is familiar in her life. She concludes that, yes, it is.

She reflects on past experiences where she felt those same feelings of being less than and concludes, "Yes, I've felt this multiple times over the years, beginning when I was in elementary school and even in previous jobs where I felt intimidated by others because of how they judged my work and valued my input. Even at home, I felt pressure from my parents and how they compared me to my siblings, who initially had better grades than I did at school and now have more successful careers. This fear of failure propels me to work harder for a promotion and to be more successful to prove myself to my family."

Once she feels the emotional pain and realizes where it comes from, she's ready to drop into her body.

She expands her awareness into the physical sensation of frustration and where it shows up in her body, and she realizes that it's right in the solar plexus, over her stomach, under her rib cage.

Now that she can locate the emotional charge in her body, she gets ready to apply the third Power Step, Welcome, and the third

Power Tool, Conscious Discomfort, to stay with the physical sensations that arise in her body.

She gently turns her attention to her solar plexus and softly investigates what's happening.

What kind of physical sensations do I feel?

Tightness and a little bit of tension.

She calmly observes these sensations.

Next, she wants to determine the intensity level of these sensations. So she tunes in and decides that her sensations are an eight on a scale from one to ten, with ten being the most intense.

Then, she queries the size of these sensations. What does this look like? How big is it? She comes up with a fruit, an apple, as its size.

I always suggest that when determining the size, it's helpful to use a type of fruit as a reference, such as a lemon, apple, grapefruit, or melon, or a type of round shape, such as a marble, golf ball, baseball, bowling ball, or basketball, because it's easier to connect the abstract physical sensations to physical, familiar, and relatable objects.

To deepen her connection with the emotional charge and its physical sensations, she probes the tightness to see what color the physical sensation in her solar plexus has, and she decides that it appears "yellow" when she visualizes it.

When determining the intensity, shape, and color of these physical sensations, she's practicing Conscious Discomfort by staying with the pain that procrastination and frustration cause in her body.

After maybe twenty to thirty seconds of staying with the Conscious Discomfort, she is now ready to release the "repressed fear of being a failure" from her body and relieve the burden from her subconscious programming. She gets ready to apply the 3-by-3 Breath without losing her connection with the physical sensation she's been consciously welcoming into her awareness.

She takes a deep breath into her solar plexus, into that tightness, and then holds her breath for three seconds. While holding her breath, she acknowledges the tightness and understands what the physical sensation represents: her fear of being a complete and utter failure. With that deep insight, she exhales the physical sensation with some force, some oomph to make some noise.

She repeats this routine two more times to complete the entire cycle of the 3-by-3 Breath.

As she completes the breath cycle, the intensity of the physical sensations gradually decreases to three. Now, she feels more empowered to take control back from her subconscious fight-or-flight defense mechanisms of watching TV or scrolling on social media and instead goes for a quick walk at a nearby park to clear her energy. When she comes home, she sits down at her desk with more clarity and motivation to work on her project.

I assume this protocol becomes second nature to me when I consistently apply it to the physical sensations I feel in my body, whenever I have an intense emotional reaction. Well, what do I do after applying the 3-by-3 Breath technique?

As you can appreciate, staying connected with the physical sensations in the body during Conscious Discomfort and 3-by-3 Breath is essential. That connection helps you process your repressed fears more effectively. You subsequently balance your emotional reactivity with the 3-by-3 Breath. You feel less charged.

In that calmer state of mind, you will be ready to explore with curiosity what happens in any trigger event. You can execute this exploration with a new Communication Strategy, which requires even more presence and higher awareness levels than the previous two.

THIRD COMMUNICATION STRATEGY: ASKING OPEN-ENDED CURIOUS QUESTIONS

In this strategy, the key to success is curiosity, and the most critical element is to ask open-ended questions using who, what, when, where, why, and how as much as you can. You want to be interested in the other person's point of view and learn where they are coming from. At the end of the day, they trigger you because they say or do something to you due to their own subconscious programming. Your job is to investigate and understand why they are doing what they're doing.

Here are some Open-Ended Curious Questions you can use as your Communication Strategy. The list is not exclusive, but it can give you some ideas and, hopefully, the freedom to ask any Open-Ended Curious Questions you'd like:

What did you mean when you said that?

What was your thought process when you responded to me?

How would you feel if something like this happened to you?

How did you feel about my reaction?

Where do you think we should go from here?

How can we address this without arguing?

Why do you think I missed that task?

What's really important to you in this situation?

How did you arrive at that conclusion?

How do you see this conflict getting resolved?

What's your viewpoint on this topic?

How does this situation affect you?

Even though this list includes some powerful questions, I highly encourage you to stay in the moment and not rely too much on remembering these exact phrases when responding to a trigger event. Once you discharge the physical sensations out of your body and reach a point of lightness with the 3-by-3 Breath, you can get into a curious state and come up with more powerful and creative questions.

Only open-ended questions? Why should I avoid using closed-ended yes-or-no questions?

Let's say someone makes a comment that offends you. You respond with anger and ask a closed-ended question, like "Is that what you think?" The other person will answer it with a straightforward "yes" or "no." Where do you go from there? The conversation is stuck. The interaction doesn't go too deep. The connection breaks down. There's not much space to build on. Everyone closes down. And as a result, you don't get much information about why they make comments that ultimately trigger you.

Instead, imagine asking an open-ended question, like "Where did that comment come from?" Now, the energy between you and the other person opens up for a deeper connection. Your curiosity allows for better information exchange and a deeper understanding of where they come from. There's now a palpable space where the conversation can deepen and hold space for meaningful interactions.

When you are curious about a person's thoughts and perspectives, they feel safe to share them with you. When you are open and sincere in your curious approach, they will not feel threatened or offended by your comments and attitudes. Therefore, you should not use Communication Strategies to win an argument, degrade others, or put down their ideas and opinions. When you stay neutral, neither defensive nor offensive, but purely curious and factual, you will enjoy establishing deep connections with people you may not have experienced before.

When I ask Open-Ended Curious Questions, others start to talk. I get anxious and want to interrupt them and explain where I'm coming from. The interaction doesn't go too far. What shall I do in these cases?

When you try to explain your point of view or justify your actions, the conversation inevitably goes south. Why? As we discussed earlier, explanations and justifications are defensive actions; as a result, they come across as offensive to the other person. When you explain yourself, you ignore their feelings. When you justify your actions, you disrespect them. They want what you want: to be heard, seen, respected, and regarded.

When you are defensive, it's challenging to connect with curiosity and genuinely ask open-ended questions. Your subconscious is not curious. It interprets a situation as a threat and fires up its fight-or-flight defense mechanisms. As simple as that. It's binary. In lower consciousness levels, life is always black and white. It's either or. Therefore, you're right that when you are in that survival mode, you are far away from curiosity and can't muster up Open-Ended Curious Questions.

The cure to this conundrum is raising your consciousness level by processing more of your repressed fears—which you have already started. Once you gain more awareness of your subconscious programming and how it controls your reactions, you will be more open to curiosity and, eventually, ask more Open-Ended Curious Questions.

To answer the second part of your question, the other person will start to talk, and they might throw out everything they've been holding back at you. I call this phenomenon "throw-up" or "verbal vomit." After asking an Open-Ended Curious Question, you need to step back and let the other person share whatever they need to share. Be courteous and hold the bucket for their throw-up so they feel comfortable fully opening up and sharing everything with you.

FOURTH COMMUNICATION STRATEGY: HOLDING SPACE WITH ATTENTIVE LISTENING

Imagine the flow of a harmonious interaction. The questions you ask and the curiosity you bring into the conversation gently invite you to execute your fourth Communication Strategy, Holding Space with Attentive Listening. As we discussed, we can also call this strategy holding the bucket for throw-ups. I hope you experience how well it fits into the conversation after you ask Open-Ended Curious Questions. After all, what do you expect when you ask someone a question? They'll answer you. You have no choice but to listen and hold space for them when their answers become verbal vomits.

Maybe you'll have another choice. You may take their throw-ups personally. Well, in that case, are you going to get defensive? Will you try to explain yourself? Will you let the whole conversation spiral down into more drama? Or are you going to regulate your emotional reactions? Can you notice your emotions, observe your thoughts, and welcome whatever is coming up in your body? Only then will you be able to consciously respond using your Communication Strategies.

Every Communication Strategy brings another set of challenges for you, where you can expand your awareness, acquire more self-knowledge, and learn more about your repressed fears. Therefore, curiosity requires higher energy levels and deeper self-awareness than expressing feelings (second strategy) or responding to triggers differently (first strategy).

At every level, Communication Strategies test your personal work. How present can you be when they start answering your "curious" questions? How well can you release the emotional charges if you get triggered? How attentively can you listen to them? How present can you stay without losing focus, getting angry, eye-rolling, or leaving the room? Since you've asked them a question, you're simply there to hold space for what they have to say.

What happens if the other person, usually my partner, doesn't want to talk about it? What if they are quiet and don't want to engage in these emotional interactions?

Yes, that happens. Now, you have the opposite problem: not getting any answers to your questions. Well, let's see what you can do when that happens. How have you been dealing with no-answer situations before? Can you respond with Doing the Opposite strategy first? Namely, stop paying attention to them and look inward instead.

Why are you getting triggered when they don't respond to you? How long can you stay silent and wait for them to speak? How much discomfort do you feel when they don't engage in the conversation? Do they remind you of someone from your past? How much attachment do you have for them to talk to you and share more? After executing your first Communication Strategy, can you express your feelings with I-Feel Statements and invite them to tell you more about what's happening with them by asking them Open-Ended Curious Questions?

By the way, the "holding the bucket" to verbal vomit is not intended to make you absorb more hurt. Conversely, you're opening the contracted space in a relationship between you and the other person who triggers you. Of course, they may want to share all their dirty laundry with you. They may tell you how uncomfortable they feel in front of you, how intimidating you are, or how controlling you become whenever they share their thoughts. But consider these throw-ups as critical moments where everybody starts to open up about what they've been holding back.

With these Communication Strategies, your interactions are bound to become more honest and open. They're thinking, "Since you asked, here is my answer—about you!" So, please keep encouraging them with "Tell me more," and hold the bucket when they start sharing everything they've been suppressing.

I hope these strategies get them to talk, no matter how quiet their nature might be. Try to consciously and attentively listen to them as they air out any grievances or resentments they've been holding against you. In some cases, you may even physically step a few inches back so they feel even more comfortable sharing safely and are not intimidated by you.

When you have thoroughly processed your repressed fears, you can execute this Holding Space with Attentive Listening strategy much more quickly and confidently. By now, you know you're not the only one with repressed fears. Everyone has them. Of course, everyone is just as vulnerable as you are and has similar sensitivities to certain words, attitudes, actions, and triggers.

After executing this strategy for a couple of days, check in with yourself. Have you been observing your interactions with others lately? Are they becoming more meaningful? Do you see now that we all want the same thing: to be heard, to be seen, to be understood, and to belong? I know it's hard to switch from being triggered to getting curious about another person's perspective and where they're coming from. But through some diligent practice, you'll be able to hold more space for others and enjoy a positive shift in your conversations.

Now that I'm taking things less personally, I can see that sometimes what they're saying is partially true. What I mean by that is they may say, "You always ignore my needs!" Yes, I realize that I have actually ignored their needs, but not always. Should I be blunt and tell them to avoid the words always, never, etc.?

No, not at all. That'll be defensive. You'll trigger them more because you ignore what they share with you. Any explanation, any justification, is defensive and will offend others. Therefore, when someone communicates in general statements like "You always ignore my needs," acknowledge that their subconscious fight-or-flight defense mechanisms are active. They're attacking you because they're already offended by your actions or lack thereof. That's why they make general, blanket statements, which are usually judgmental, even though they may carry some truth.

In these cases, right at the moment of such throw-up, pause and observe your thoughts to evaluate if what the other person is saying is even partially true. Suppose you don't understand what they're referring to. In that case, you can go back and apply the third Communication Strategy and ask an Open-Ended Curious Question to find out more about their general statements.

However, if there is a part of you who partially agrees that what they're saying has some validity, then it's time to apply the fifth Communication Strategy, Leveling with an Aikido Move. In this strategy, you basically admit the truth in their statement and give them an example of a situation that validates their statement to hear what they're sharing and acknowledge and recognize their position.

FIFTH COMMUNICATION STRATEGY: LEVELING WITH AN AIKIDO MOVE

In my opinion, this Communication Strategy is the most difficult one among the seven you'll be practicing as part of your Emotional Mastery training. Let me explain why.

Do you know what an Aikido Move is?

Aikido is a modern Japanese martial art where the attacker's forceful attempt to harm is controlled and redirected by the receiver's energy without too much effort. The receiver understands the attacker's intent and finds a solid foundation to counter the attacker's movement with a grounded and centered stance. The receiver discharges the harmful attack, or the trigger, without combative or defensive action. They harmoniously flow with their opponent's force and movements and direct them to the floor.

Does this remind you of our emotional regulation techniques? Do you see the resemblance to how it almost describes the 5-Step Power Method in martial arts terms? The underlying principles are "avoiding combat or rising above conflict" and "pacifying opponents' offenses" through harmonious interactions.

Therefore, as a Communication Strategy, Leveling with an Aikido Move meets a trigger without exerting energy, defensive effort, or combativeness. In some cases, using this strategy means relating to the intensity of others' emotional reactions, going with the flow no matter how much they blame you, ignoring their verbal attacks as you see and understand them as a projection of their own repressed fears, gently rolling with the names they call you, or staying present and emotionally detached from their unreasonable acts or exaggerated role-play.

Leveling with an Aikido Move is designed solely for you to protect your boundaries and ward off attackers and triggers by maintaining your energy and not getting emotionally involved with hurtful conflicts and fruitless arguments. At the same time, you neutralize the other person's verbal attack or offense through acceptance and acknowledgment. This technique aims to realize and eventually overcome one's own agenda and ego attachments while creating a harmonious flow for you and others through effective and open communication.

No matter how much we try, relationships can sometimes become power struggles. Who's right, who's wrong? Who triggered whom? Whose fault is it? In a sense, in every interaction like this between two people, both carry their own agenda. They want to prove their point to the other person and maintain their position and posture against the other person's goal.

These exchanges become endless arguments because they're defensive moves that snowball into back-and-forth offensive attacks. These types of interactions create fruitless conflicts about who has more power or more say over things, who overpowers whom, who directs the activity in the household, at work, in friends' groups, and so on.

When Leveling with an Aikido Move, the trick is to remain neutral and factual by staying in the body and connected with your physical sensations so you can release them using 3-by-3 Breath. This constant application of the Power Method allows you to gauge where others are and meet them at their level. Always remember that you're not above them, nor should you be intimidated by them. You're simply there to observe what's happening and what they're saying. After you defuse the emotional charge out of your body, it's ultimately your call to agree or disagree with what they're sharing with you.

What is your style? What is your persona during these conflict-ridden interactions?

Do you usually try to fix other people's problems?

Or alternatively, are you the one who quickly apologizes for mistakes?

Are you a controller, telling people what to do or how to behave, or are you a conflict avoider, staying quiet and passive not to rock the boat?

Some of us identify ourselves as fixers, people pleasers, approval seekers, or conflict avoiders. When we carry such personalities, it becomes somewhat difficult to apply the Leveling with an Aikido Move strategy. In those situations, try listening to others more carefully and attentively. They may not be asking you to fix their problem, meet their needs, or apologize for the conflict. They may just want to be heard, seen, and held by you.

When you pause and observe what's happening, can you gently hold space for them without imposing your own agenda, giving them advice to make them feel better, forcing your point of view on them, shutting down to avoid further arguments, or running away from unpleasant conversations? Instead, can you simply listen to what they have to say and offer encouragement to share and clarify even more?

The bottom line is whatever you do, try to maintain your curiosity and keep asking clarifying questions. Then, attentively listen to their answer and respectfully receive their perspective about what's going on so that you set yourself up for a successful execution of an Aikido Move. Through this practice of attentive listening, you'll be surprised by how connected you feel with others, even though they just triggered you moments ago by sharing their dirty laundry.

You may want to really master the 3-by-3 Breath before you attempt this advanced Communication Strategy. If you can't use the Aikido Move, you can go back to I-Feel Statements and defuse the situation by simply saying, "I feel attacked" or "I feel hurt" or using a more elaborate response such as, "I feel confused as I'm hearing some of this for the first time." Then, follow up with an Open-Ended Curious Question: "Why didn't we talk about these before? How do you feel about sharing your thoughts about this situation?"

Applying this strategy can be tricky and requires good training. The key to successfully executing the Aikido Move is to leave your ego behind, advocate for yourself with I-Feel Statements, and deploy your Open-Ended Curious Questions when necessary. Because you're not being asked to defend yourself, meaning you're leaving your ego and repressed fears behind, you need to apply the 3-by-3 Breath technique to level with the person who just triggered you.

I feel like by using these strategies, I can form better relationships, not just at home but at work as well. To help me grasp some of these concepts, can you share a few more examples of using them in different situations?

Let's review the following three scenarios. Please note that from here on out, you can interchangeably use any Communication Strategies we've reviewed against your triggers. However, the only caveat is to use them only after staying in Conscious Discomfort for a short while and after applying the 3-by-3 Breath to process your repressed fears.

When you release the emotional charge out of your body, your success rate tremendously increases and helps you set healthy boundaries with others. In the following scenarios, please consider how all five Communication Strategies are used interchangeably. Each strategy builds on the previous one and helps you expand your awareness and form healthy boundaries.

Scenario One

The Trigger: Rachel has been on the dating scene for a few months now and is increasingly frustrated with the guys she seems to attract. She wonders, *Why do I only attract the guys who turn out to be wrong for me when my friends match up with these amazing studs?!* Every time Rachel meets a new guy, she gets hopeful. Her bubbly, magnetic personality draws guys in immediately, making her feel special from the attention. But by the fourth or fifth day, the heat of the connection cools off and the guy usually stops texting her or communicates infrequently. On the next date, the conversation flows less, and the spark fades as the dates eventually end.

Emotions: Rachel experiences anxiety and annoyance with herself for attracting these noncommittal guys. She starts worrying about how she will find her Mr. Right if she keeps dating these losers and feels disappointed about the lack of serious, available men.

Thoughts: Rachel thinks there's no one for her. She's losing faith in her ability to find a committed partner and imagines she might be driving men away with her flaws.

Feelings: Rachel feels not good enough, unworthy of commitment, and abandoned by life.

Repressed Fears: Rachel realizes these feelings have been a common theme in her life, especially after her parents' divorce.

Origins: Rachel remembers her parents' nasty divorce when she was six and how she spent long stretches with her grandmother, feeling lonely. Her parents left her with her mom's mom and started living separately, taking her with them one weekend at a time. She felt so lonely in those days that she started making friends with almost everybody to avoid staying at home with her grandma. She was part of many friendship cliques. Once she made those friendships, she felt connected to other people, and she stuffed her parents' divorce and how lonely she felt back then deep down inside.

Physical Sensations: Rachel's anxiety, disappointment, and worry manifest all in one area in her belly. When she doesn't hear from a guy after a promising fourth date with no follow-up, the intensity of those physical sensations goes up to eight. She characterizes the sensations as like a grapefruit, colored brown, but does not know why.

Old Reaction: After each rejection, Rachel shuts down, shies away from dating, and distracts herself by going out with friends to forget about the guy. For a while, she tells herself that she detests the whole dating scene, the fakeness of online dating apps, and everything and everyone who rejected her in the past. Eventually, her loneliness gets the better of her, and she reactivates her profile and tries again until she runs into her usual pattern.

New Response: Yet another guy, yet another rejection. One night, while she's thinking about the fifth date she's had with a new crush, the guy calls her and says, "You're a great girl, Rachel, but I don't feel the vibe anymore. But can we stay friends? By the way, have you ever worked on your commitment issues with your therapist?"

After they hang up, Rachel initially gets angry at the guy for his bluntness, but this time, she realizes she may be the one with emotional issues rooted in her childhood feelings of abandonment. Through some more reflection, it comes to her that she may have commitment issues after all. She realizes that she needs to apply Doing the Opposite and face her fears to turn things around.

It takes a few days for her to gather her courage; this time, she's determined to open up and feel the discomfort of potentially committing to a relationship. She returns to the dating app to look for someone to go out with. During her first date with this new guy, she applies Doing the Opposite to its full extent. For example, even though her default behavior is cheerful, flirtatious, and seductive, she settles down. She calmly uses I-Feel statements to describe herself, her feelings, and her dating experiences. Now and then, she asks the new guy Open-Ended Curious Questions, as she genuinely gets into an energy of curiosity and intention of getting to know him.

After the date, Rachel doesn't get anxious or triggered when the new guy doesn't respond to her text for a few days. On the next date, Rachel decides to hold more space for this new guy by asking more questions instead of trying to highlight and share her own merits. As he feels more comfortable with her, he opens up and starts sharing his I-Feel Statements about the whole dating experience and his life. He tells her how he feels bad enough when he compares himself to other guys. He shares how his insecurities may be coming from his relationship with his dad.

As he shares more intimate details about himself, he senses the space Rachel holds for him. He feels courageous and confident to ask

Rachel questions about her life and her previous dating experience. His questions make Rachel feel special as he displays a new level of interest and curiosity in her, unlike the other men she's dated. She feels the magic of holding space and smiles because, through acceptance of her own fear with an Aikido Move, she was able to ignite new interactions and have a higher-quality conversation with this new guy. Even though it is a mellow and slow start, the connection seems deeper than the other dates she's gone on. Rachel starts to feel hopeful that her new understanding of herself will improve her life. This feeling of new beginnings makes her less anxious and lonely, even though she doesn't know where this new relationship will go.

Scenario Two

The Trigger: Becky loves being a mom. She treasures every moment she spends with her two-year-old daughter, Ashley. Yet she has a nagging feeling that having a second child would be great. However, her husband doesn't want to have another child, and this difference in preference causes them to get into fights that make them question the future of their relationship.

Emotions: Becky experiences anxiety about her relationship and her daughter's future and disappointment in her husband for not seeing her needs as well as caring for their daughter.

Thoughts: Becky thinks her husband dedicates too much time to his work and hobbies and doesn't invest in the relationship and what their connection requires of them.

Feelings: She feels misunderstood, disregarded, and lonely because her husband is unwilling to budge on his decision not to have a second child.

Repressed Fears: Fear of being a bad, uncaring mother, of being treated as though her opinion doesn't matter, and of being lonely because her husband has threatened to leave if she insists on having a second baby.

Origins: As Becky goes through the reverse engineering process, she remembers how difficult it was witnessing her parents' divorce when she was seven. As an only child, she was close to her parents and didn't want them to separate. She didn't have a close circle of relatives to support her during these situations. Now, at the age of twenty-eight and worried about her relationship with her husband, she recalls feeling lonely and having no one to lean on for her emotional support. She wished she had a sibling like she did when she was seven, to call family and share her true, intimate feelings with them. She's afraid her daughter will experience similar feelings of agony and despair when she grows up.

Physical Sensations: Every time she gets into an argument with her husband about whether they should have another child, Becky feels intense heaviness in her chest, which she characterizes as a level nine. For some reason, she always pictures the heavy sensation as a watermelon, and the color she sees is always black.

Old Reaction: Becky usually shuts down and doesn't want to talk to her husband ever again. Of course, she cools down afterward, and things return to normal, but she's always reactive to her husband when he wants to do something for himself. Becky feels the resentment is already building as she doesn't give her husband enough space and feels constricted by his uncompromising position.

New Response: After these deep reflections on her emotional reactions and the origins of her repressed fears, Becky decides to do something different. One night, after their daughter goes to bed, she invites her husband to the sofa. She turns the TV off and says, "I know it's been a pretty tough couple of months. We've been arguing intensely. You know what I want, right? I only want to support our daughter if something happens to us or our relationship. I want her to feel safe and not lonely in this world. But I feel shut down every time I suggest that. I'm trying to do something for my daughter that she'll be thankful for later in life. How does having another child make you feel?"

Becky steps back a few inches to hold space for her husband as she prepares to listen attentively and curiously to what he has to say. On the other hand, Becky's husband is surprised by the emotional intimacy she brings into the conversation, especially with her Open-Ended Curious Questions. So he tries to match it, and this time, he feels safe telling her how he feels. He says, "Becky, sweetie, I know why you want another baby. You've told me about your parents and why you react the way you do. You know my story also. I experienced the challenges and difficulties my parents faced after they had their third kid. You see how busy I am at work. You take on the brunt of housework. I can't help you with anything. I'm afraid having the second child for the sake of our daughter's safety and as a future cure for her loneliness will make our marriage fall apart. You'll be exhausted. I'll be exhausted."

Becky backs off a bit more to create more space for him and herself to reflect on her husband's words. *Could he be right?* she thinks contemplatively. She levels with him with an Aikido Move and says, "I hear you. The second child could be the end of their marriage. I focused on what I needed but didn't think through for our marriage. You're right; caring for a new baby requires time and energy, which neither of us has much these days. But, how could I let go of such desire to support our daughter with a sibling?" As she tries to see it from her husband's point of view, she wants to explore the topic a little bit more. She follows her Open-Ended Curious Question with another: "So tell me, how did it affect you as a kid when you saw your parents struggle to deal with three kids?" He tells her he felt abandoned when his parents had their third kid, as their love got wholly redirected to the newborn. Even though their situation is different, Becky suddenly realizes why her husband works so hard and dedicates so much to his hobbies. He might feel abandoned by her as most of her attention goes to her daughter.

After gaining such a deep understanding of her husband, Becky does one more Aikido Move and says, "I see what you mean; how about we reflect on this a little bit more? But I understand where you're coming from, and I'll think more deeply about my desire to have a second child. Thank you for sharing your thoughts with me." With this acceptance and openness, Becky takes the tension out of the conversation and deepens the connection by lifting the pressure off her husband. They don't resolve anything that night, but it is a moment of emotional intimacy they have never felt before. They both sleep very deeply and soundly that night.

Scenario Three

The Trigger: Andrew finds himself rushing to work almost every morning. As he's driving in rush hour traffic, he wonders when he will get a grip on his time management and get out of the house at a reasonable time. He always gets stressed when running late, as he runs into all sorts of traffic issues, accidents, and angry drivers. Also, he gets stuck behind the slowest driver on the freeway almost every morning. He often thinks to himself, *It should be illegal to drive this slow in the fast lane!* This results in him consistently showing up late to his morning meeting and being embarrassed in front of his team. As he walks into the room, they all seem to have mocking grins as if to say, "Again, boss?!"

Emotions: Andrew is extremely frustrated with himself and his lack of discipline with time management. On top of that, he's embarrassed to be in front of his team. He's supposed to be the one in charge, but instead, he looks like an incompetent manager every time. Who is he if he can't manage his time—especially when he runs late to his *own* staff meeting?

Thoughts: Andrew thinks he's a loser who can't get his act together. He's not competent enough to leave home ten minutes early. Of course, when starting his day late, he feels obligated to stay at work longer than the others to prove he's not slacking. These thoughts make him feel even more guilty because he's pretending to stay late, but he doesn't do much work because he chats around with others to pass the time as they all wind down at the end of the day.

Feelings: Andrew feels inadequate and incapable of doing simple things to improve his life. He also feels like a failure when he looks at his apartment. His dating life and work performance all lack the momentum he craves. Nothing seems to work for him or goes his way, so he feels unworthy of anything.

Repressed Fear: These themes are so familiar to Andrew that he quickly decides he fears not being good enough and not having any worth. He also realizes that he believes he hasn't lived up to his parent's expectations regarding his career and personal life. He's still single and is only a senior director, while most of his friends are happily married and have achieved executive-level positions where they run large teams.

Origins: As Andrew starts his reverse engineering process, following the thread from his emotions of self-deprecating anger to his thoughts of being a failure and loser, he realizes that he always felt tense and anxious when he was growing up. He was expected to be a golden child due to his dad's prominence in business. His dad provided constant mentorship and encouraged him to go to Ivy League schools to set his future on the right track. Andrew was also able to take advantage of opportunities that he got through his dad's connections. Now, looking back and assessing what he's feeling right now, Andrew didn't realize how much pressure he was under to perform at a high level and how much he was falling short of his dad's expectations, making him feel not good enough, and maybe even more than that, like a non-achiever. Now that his dad is no longer around, his inner voice replaces his dad's in pushing him to do more and putting himself down for not being a more stand-up, put-together guy.

Physical Sensations: Andrew notices he has sharp stabbing pain in his shoulders and between his shoulder blades at an intensity level of seven. He visualizes the pain as the size of a lemon and in a dark green color. As Andrew reflects on these sensations, it dawns on him that he's been carrying this heavy weight on his shoulders, the physical manifestation of the pressure from his parents, especially his dad, for decades. He uses the 3-by-3 Breath, and his powerful, almost scream-like exhale brings the intensity down to two in the first cycle. After this, he feels sleepy and goes to bed early. His body keeps processing the tightness and his repressed fears of being a failure throughout the night. The following morning, he wakes up feeling a little bit lighter and more refreshed than other days.

Old Reaction: Andrew learns a lot from his introspection into his childhood and how he became the person he is today. His emotional reactions to others come from being exhausted and depleted by his inner critic, who constantly berates him for being such a dud. As he learns about the origins of his repressed fears, Andrew realizes that he overloads his schedule with many things to do so that he feels good about himself.

But no matter what he does, he always ends up feeling like a failure because there's not enough time to do everything he needs to be successful and become the golden child his dad wanted. When he tries to do it all, he feels completely exhausted and demotivated, making him not want to do anything, which leads to procrastination. As a result, he stays up late at night, spending time on social media or the internet to soothe his feelings of being a washout. Then, he remains in bed longer in the mornings because he's tired from the previous night, which makes him hit the road later than he wants. As a result, he gets stuck in busy morning traffic and runs late to his morning meetings. He hates himself on the way to work as he can't seem to get his act together to break this cycle.

New Response: Andrew says, "That's it! Tomorrow is the day I will get up at a reasonable time, finish my morning routine, and get on the road in time to beat rush hour traffic and appear at work a few minutes before my first meeting!" He feels good about his decision and realizes the whole routine starts the night before. He recognizes his urge to procrastinate and not go to bed on time. He uses an I-Feel Statement on himself, saying, "I feel like a failure, an idiot, not following my promise to myself to go to bed early." Right after that, he remembers to ask an Open-Ended Curious Question. "Why do I sabotage myself?" The first thought that comes to his mind is the feeling he had when his dad scolded him for not doing the things he expected him to accomplish.

Andrew thinks, *What if I go to bed right now, so what? What would happen?* He has so much more to achieve and not enough time! He wants to meet his dad's expectations. Right then, he puts himself together, goes to the bathroom, washes his face, brushes his teeth, picks up a book instead of opening his laptop, and goes to bed. He feels discomfort but uses the 3-by-3 Breath to defuse the emotional charge that is building up in his body. He repeats the breath work one more time. Finally, he starts to feel tired. He doesn't need to prove himself to his dad, himself, his boss, or anybody else anymore. The day is finally over. The pressure is off.

He has never realized that all he does is try to prove himself to others. His eyes are opened to the truth that everything he did was for his dad. With that revelation, his body feels even more tired, and the book in his hands falls to the floor, waking him up just enough to turn his bedside lamp off. He nods off with a relaxed grin as he promises himself not to look at the dark, loser, failure side of him ever again.

JOURNAL ENTRY FOR WEEK THREE

For the next seven days, make a journal entry at the end of each day to capture the most intense trigger event that occurred. Do this review by answering the following questions:

1. What was the trigger event?
2. What emotions did you experience?
3. What thoughts did you have?
4. What were your feelings?
5. Can you identify your repressed fears?
6. What are their origins?
7. What physical sensations did you experience?
8. What is your typical reaction?
9. What will be your new Communication Strategy?

DAILY CHECKLIST FOR WEEK THREE

1. Have you practiced the following Power Steps?

    - Pause to notice your emotions.
    - Observe your thoughts.
    - Welcome your physical sensations.

2. Have you practiced the following techniques?

    - Square Breathing
    - Self-Observation Meditation
    - 3-by-3 Breath

3. Have you practiced the following tools?

    - I'm {the emotion}
    - What If—So What
    - Conscious Discomfort

4. Have you used any of the following Communication Strategies?

    - Doing the Opposite
    - Using I-Feel Statements
    - Asking Open-Ended Curious Questions
    - Holding Space with Attentive Listening
    - Leveling with an Aikido Move

CHAPTER FIVE

MOVING FROM CHAOS TO CALM

Grounding the Emotional Intensity

It's another typical weekday morning, and things are pretty hectic. You're trying to prepare breakfast, but the kids are dragging their feet. They're not even dressed yet. You're anxiously keeping an eye on the clock. The school bell is going to ring in forty-five minutes, and if you left in ten minutes, you could barely make it. When you think about how on earth you'll leave the house on time, one of your kids starts to scream. They can't find their favorite jacket. Oh, don't forget to pack their lunches. Stress is mounting, and you can feel yourself about to lose your composure as the morning madness unfolds.

You're not alone. Most of us experience such crazy mornings, day after day. The chaos feels like a category-five hurricane when we're in it. I'm sure craziness of such magnitude doesn't only exist in the mornings at home during the school rush. It's everywhere. Take a second to reflect upon the pandemonium of big family gatherings, inviting friends over for dinners, team meetings, project deadlines, and trying to get to events on time in rush hours; they may all feel like you're lost in a storm, completely uprooted, like a loose leaf in the wind.

Do you have to feel like you're spiraling out of control whenever you experience these situations? Understandably, the stakes are high, so it's easy to get caught up in the stress and let it take over. But what if you could handle that energy differently and find some calm in the chaos? What if we explored another step in the Power Method that would make you feel like you're in the eye of the storm, calm and centered? What if this Power Step could help you get rooted and grounded on earth like a tree?

You're about to learn your fourth Power Step, called Earth. This profound, almost life-changing step will help you anywhere where you're lost in the wind with intense emotional reactions. I hope you can already imagine how such grounded and centered energy can make even the craziest mornings feel more manageable. Whatever the out-of-control situation may be, staying cool and collected through it all will make you feel in charge. As a result, you will tune into a more harmonious flow, bringing some peace to your hectic day and your busy mind.

I experience this and many other things daily. I have too much craziness going on in my life. I need this! How do I use this fourth Power Step along with other steps?

To earth intense emotional reactions is an essential step that beautifully integrates the first three steps you've been practicing. I'm pretty sure you've already noticed I use *earth* as a verb. You use this step to ground the emotional charge by diverting it to the ground. You can use this process to ground the static electricity to protect your house from electrical overloads. Your body is your house. In simple terms, earthing discharges the emotional intensity you feel as physical sensations into the earth through the bottoms of your feet.

You can apply this fourth Power Step right after you use the 3-by-3 Breath. As you'll recall, you first locate the emotional charge, the physical sensations your emotions create due to a trigger event. Then, you inhale into that part of your body, knowing where your repressed fears are located, and exhale the discomfort out of your mouth.

Earthing fits right into that exhale, requiring a quick adaptation from you. When exhaling the physical sensations out of your mouth, turn your focus to the bottoms of your feet. When you feel the ground underneath your feet while still exhaling, imagine letting the physical sensations go out of your body into the floor, the ground, and the earth. That's exactly what it means to earth.

As I mentioned earlier, you're grounding the static electricity, the emotional charge that your fight-or-flight defense mechanism creates in your body as a response to a trigger. You must bring your awareness to the bottoms of your feet every time you exhale. Your body follows your breath and your attention and consciously pushes the physical sensations out of your mouth while you release the emotional charge to the earth at the same time.

You may literally feel energy flowing out of your body into the ground. Some of my clients sense this movement of energy as tingling, heat, or heaviness on the bottoms of their feet. Of course, every person is different. See how you feel when you're doing it. But I assure you that if you can focus on both—exhaling out of your mouth and grounding through the bottoms of your feet—you will experience some shift in your body.

After the third exhale, keep your focus on the bottoms of your feet for an extended period—ideally for a few seconds if you're applying the Power Method to a trigger event in real-time or for two or three minutes if you're doing this exercise as part of your Daily Review practice at the end of the day.

In either case, gently tune into your body after the 3-by-3 Breath and listen to what's happening there. Observe the calmness settling in as you connect with the floor, with the ground underneath your feet. Then, slowly bring your awareness to the part of your body where you spotted the emotional charge earlier. How does the intensity of those physical sensations feel right now? Are they as high as before you applied the 3-by-3 Breath? Can you sense some lightness in your body?

If not, and you still feel the intensity of the physical sensations at a three or above, please do the 3-by-3 Breath again, maybe this time establishing a more profound connection by keeping your focus on the intensity, size, and color of your physical sensations a little longer before letting them go out of your body. In addition to sharpening your concentration, you can deepen your understanding of your repressed fears and how they connect with the physical sensations you're trying to exhale and release to the earth.

FOURTH POWER TECHNIQUE: GROUNDING

Staying connected to the bottoms of your feet after your third exhale is a very important practice. Your fourth Power Technique is called Grounding. You apply this technique by focusing on the bottom of your feet and keeping your attention on the floor underneath you. Would you like to try it now? Wherever you are—at your desk, on an airplane, on a bench at the park, waiting in line at the grocery store, or stuck in traffic—tap into the sensation of your feet on the ground. Do you sense a subtle shift in your energy?

Through every trigger and blow, keep trying to ground that static emotional intensity by discharging the physical sensations into the earth using the 3-by-3 Breath and bringing your attention to the bottoms of your feet. And every time you do that, you'll feel more and more stable. When you use this Power Technique, you allow the earth's energy to help you neutralize the emotional charge in your body so that you feel steadier and can appropriately respond to triggers and not get hooked and lost in your emotional reactions to them.

By building this strong foundation, you start to take more control over your automatic fight-or-flight defense mechanisms, which are the culprits that keep you in the chaos. When you take the charge back from your subconscious, you feel more empowered and present in any given moment. Every ounce of power you regain means you're getting closer to emotional mastery.

Why is the grounding technique so effective? How does this energetic shift happen every time I ground myself?

When you're acting under the influence of your subconscious programming, you live in your head. You constantly think about your day and everything you have to do and take care of—emails to respond to, kids to pick up, dinners to cook, meetings to go to, errands to run, and so on. What happens when you live in your head like this all day?

Do you remember the phrase we used earlier? Energy flows where your attention goes. Thus, if your attention is always in your head and lost in your thoughts, your energy flows there and gets stuck. All that energy makes your thoughts run at a thousand miles an hour. Even when you're not doing anything stressful, check in with yourself to see how your head feels. Heavy? Contracted? Tense? Do you have the beginnings of a headache?

No problem if you do. Most of us are in your position, feeling the intensity in our heads. But now, you have a technique. This grounding practice can profoundly change your life by supporting your mental and emotional well-being. Its benefits will help you slowly but surely get out of chaos and enter a state of calmness and groundedness for years to come.

FOURTH POWER TOOL: EXHALING OUT OF THE FEET

Here's some good news! You're finally ready to exhale the intense emotional reactions and their respective physical sensations out of your feet! With this new fourth Power Tool, Exhaling Out of the Feet, you're well equipped to use the full application of the 5-Step Power Method. As a result, you don't have to live in your head anymore. By adding this tool to your 3-by-3 Breath, you will soon experience more comfort and peace in your head, if not today, tomorrow, if not tomorrow, next week—as long as you practice. Who knows, maybe you even start experiencing fewer and fewer headaches.

As you become more familiar with the Grounding technique, you'll be more adept at exhaling these highly intensive emotional charges out of your body during a 3-by-3 Breath. When you simultaneously bring your attention and awareness to the bottoms of your feet while exhaling, you allow the energy, the static emotional intensity, to flow out of your head and out of your body into the earth.

This connects, or, I should say, plugs, your entire body into the earth. Then what happens? The energy that was stuck in your head is now spread evenly throughout your body, which immediately eliminates the frantic, hectic survival nature that comes from your subconscious fight-or-flight defense mechanisms and creates mental space by calming the intense and negative thoughts in your head.

What Communication Strategy do I use after releasing the intense emotional charge into the earth?

With every pause, with every observation, with every welcome, with every earth, in other words, every time you apply the Power Method, you're building a solid foundation, step by step, brick by brick. View this foundation as the platform from which you launch your Communication Strategies. When you have that grounded feeling, you can rise above any trigger and defuse its offense by staying centered and grounded without getting consumed by it.

It's hard to describe what happens in words. You need to practice it to feel it. Through Grounding, you basically expand the time and space between a trigger event and your emotional reaction. That's where you get your power back and achieve emotional mastery. As the time slows down and the space expands, you take control back from your subconscious programming. You have to experience this shift in real time to fully understand it. Can you imagine having conscious control over your actions to choose specific Communication Strategies that replace your typical, habitual fight-or-flight defense mechanisms?

SIXTH COMMUNICATION STRATEGY: USING I-NEED STATEMENTS

In this strategy, all you have to do is turn your repressed fears into needs. It's a straightforward concept, yet difficult to put into practice. Let's say your repressed fear is not being good enough. Then what is it you need? Your I-Need Statement. "I need to be good enough." You can phrase this need in a variety of ways in your interactions with others: "I'd like to be . . . want to be . . . desire to be . . . good enough for you."

Communicating your needs to those who trigger you will make you feel even more vulnerable. That's the only natural way to achieve emotional mastery. You're opening yourself up to further exposure of your insecurities, especially to someone who's a seemingly difficult, annoying, abusive, triggering person.

But remember, you must use your sixth Communication Strategy only after you have practiced all the previous tools, techniques, and strategies for several weeks. This is so you build up your energy and foundation to apply a new approach requiring higher awareness and a stronger presence. In the higher levels of consciousness, you can afford to be more vulnerable and sensitive and use more advanced Communication Strategies. This phenomenon occurs due to lesser ego attachments to outcome.

When you try I-Need Statements, you will naturally be afraid of retaliation, further abuse, or more challenges from those who have triggered emotional wounds in you. However, to resolve these conflicts, you must stand up for your needs and articulate them so they hear you. The more you apply this strategy, the more empowered you feel in your interactions with others. Take your time and be patient when using your I-Need Statements.

In addition to your repressed fears, there's another resource you can utilize to come up with your I-Need Statements. You may be surprised about this, but your ongoing, daily complaints indicate a deep need or a secret want you're afraid to express. Maybe you carry some kind of angst about being ridiculed, put down, or dismissed. Therefore, you would rather keep your desires hidden inside your heart than share them with your partner or others. These unmet, unexpressed desires eventually become complaints and affect your emotional reactions.

I hope you soon realize that every complaint has a corresponding unmet need. When you can see that, you can start to pause every time you complain. Once you give yourself time and space to observe the thoughts behind your complaints, you can glimpse your unmet needs. Right there and then, you can drop into your body and locate where you feel the intense physical sensations of your complaints. When you do that, you apply the 3-by-3 Breath and release the related emotional charge to feel more grounded.

After you ground yourself, look at the situation and investigate why you complain. Stay calm as you slowly determine what you want to have happen. What's missing here? What's your wish? What's important to you in this instance? What would you like to see? What do you care about the most?

Once you connect with your deeper needs, desires, and wishes, articulate them through an I-Need Statement without putting any demands on the other person. This is very important. Please do not present any demand or ask for a behavior change from the other person. If you do, it'll water down your I-Need Statements, as such words will put you back on the defense. Always remember that these Communication Strategies are for expressing what's repressed. That's your number one priority. The rest will sort itself out as you perfect how you communicate these strategies to others.

For example, let's say you and your spouse disagree on how to raise your kids, and you clash during certain situations. Your spouse wants to tell the kids what to do so that they learn. Your approach is more of an empowerment style; you want the kids to learn from their mistakes. As a result, you come across as more tolerant, while your spouse might seem more controlling.

Yes, you can blame your partner and complain about them not truly understanding parenting intricacies. You can feel not heard and not respected. All of these are valid feelings. Yet what is your real complaint here? Maybe it is that the kids are not being raised in an empowered way.

At lower consciousness levels, you will be ready to pick a fight with your spouse and try to prove that your way of raising your kids is better than theirs. You will want to beat your partner in an argument and get them to hear your perspective and see that you're right. Applying such fight-or-flight defense mechanisms will make you sound offensive and unintentionally cross your partner's boundaries.

During the application of the sixth Communication Strategy, I-Need Statements, you may want to stay more neutral, objective, and matter-of-fact so you can articulate your perspective more assertively. You see how, with this strategy, you start to detach yourself from the situation and reflect on what you really want.

In this scenario, your I-Need Statement can be something like this:

"I'd like to give the kids more autonomy to make their own decisions, even if it means they fail sometimes."

Let's see what your partner says about that. Maybe they'll disagree with you and start arguing that their parenting style is better than yours.

Then maybe you switch strategies and use the third Communication Strategy, Open-Ended Curious Questions, and reply, "Why? How is your parenting style better?"

If your partner shares their perspective openly, listen to them and hold space for their point of view. In the exchange, you learn more about how they decide their approach to parenting is better and more effective than yours. Now, you can share your thoughts and ideas with I-Feel Statements and give more examples about your approach.

What happens when we keep exchanging ideas, but the conversation doesn't go anywhere? What strategy do I use to break that loop?

You use the seventh Communication Strategy to break these stalemate situations where both parties are unwilling to budge. This strategy solves this issue by bringing everybody together and inviting them to solve any conflict for the mutual benefit of everyone with a collaborative spirit.

Such a grand goal of a mutual resolution may sound like a utopic dream to you. You're not wrong. We both know very well what usually happens after you express your needs. Resistance! More often than not, you hear from the other person something like, "What do you mean you need? I have needs, too!"

When that happens, you have five other Communication Strategies at your disposal. You could say, "Tell me more," to apply the Holding Space with Attentive Listening strategy, or ask an Open-Ended Curious Question, "What kind of unmet needs do you have?" As you gather more information about their repressed fears, you could agree with their assessment by using the Leveling with an Aikido Move strategy.

Yet again, you need that seventh Communication Strategy to instigate a more collaborative approach to problem-solving in your interactions with others. Stay even more curious and open in this last but most effective Communication Strategy. As you become more inquisitive of new possibilities, you'll enhance your conversation and deepen your connection.

SEVENTH COMMUNICATION STRATEGY: ASKING COLLABORATIVE WE QUESTIONS

With this strategy, you want to create a productive, original, mutually beneficial conflict resolution protocol between you and others. Therefore, the Collaborative We Questions strategy is about asking solution-based questions that invite others to collaborate with you in making and agreeing on helpful and beneficial decisions for everyone involved.

Here are two Collaborative We Questions to illustrate what I'm talking about. For example, when Mary complained about not having enough quality time with her husband, she asked him, "How would we both make sure that we spend enough quality time with each other?" In another example, when Marc didn't like the micromanaging style of his boss, he expressed his concern with an I-Feel Statement, followed by a Collaborative We Question, finishing with an Open-Ended Curious Question, "Hi Boss, in some projects, I don't feel empowered to make decisions on my own. How can we work together so that I have more freedom to choose the next steps? What would you recommend?"

Since you're the one studying emotional mastery, you're in charge of asking these questions. It's your responsibility to lead the conversation with curiosity and openness, inviting others to work with you on creating acceptable solutions. Of course, to have amicable resolutions, both parties must comprise to a degree. When you understand where the other person is coming from, you can tune in to what kind of solution they may be willing to accept.

My client, Fred, was struggling to create physical intimacy with his wife, Nancy. They came to me together as a couple. A few sessions later, after they had learned the Power Method and the complete set of Communication Strategies, I invited them to act out a real conversation they had had during the week. Of course, the topic was the lack of physical intimacy. The following dialogue is taken from this role play, using most strategies. Can you spot them?

Fred: "Hey, sweetie, I mentioned this to you before and would like to bring it up again. I feel like we haven't been physically intimate for a while. I'd like to have sex more frequently so that I can feel connected to you.

Nancy: Hang on a second. Are you blaming me for the lack of intimacy between us? Well, you know how busy I've been at work the last couple of months. Honey, when I hear this, I feel ignored and not valued. I know you want more sex. But what about my needs?

Fred: Oh, I see. You're right, I don't know what you need. I've been focusing on what I've missed in our relationship lately. So tell me. What are your needs?

Nancy: You know, when I'm stressed and worn out, I find that I need some personal time to recharge. Once I'm feeling more like myself, though, I'd love to hang out and have some quality time together. I know that frequency is super important to you, but for me, it's not about how often we're intimate. It's more about the quality of our intimacy.

It's not that I don't want to have sex—I'd just enjoy doing things before sex. I like snuggling up to watch a movie, grabbing some ice cream, taking a walk around the block holding hands, or even dancing to a slow song in the living room before jumping to bed and having sex. I guess what I'm saying is that I need more foreplay. I'd like to connect with you and get in the mood. Those moments will feel so intimate and special to me.

Fred: Hmm, this is eye-opening for me. I always feel rejected when you want to take more time to connect with me. I think something is wrong with me, or you don't find me attractive anymore. Maybe you are no longer interested in me. Now, what you're saying makes sense. Maybe we can try incorporating more of what you need, like more intimate time together and sharing experiences to deepen our connection. How would you feel about that?

Nancy: I'd love that. And I'm happy to work on being open to having sex more frequently as long as we incorporate some sensual foreplay into our intimacy. When I'm in the mood, I'd love to connect with you physically. I still find you sexy, my love. How about planning some date nights when we're both relaxed and can fully enjoy each other's company?

Fred: That sounds like a plan. How about we set aside specific times each week or maybe every other week to focus on making intimacy fulfilling for both of us? What do you think about Friday nights?

Nancy: Fridays are tricky. You know how busy it gets at work at times. How about we try this Saturday night? Let's not make any long-term plans. Let's see how our first one goes. I'd love to dress up, though. Where would you like to take us?

Fred: I already feel very excited about you wearing something sexy. Yay, I'm feeling good. I'm going on a date with my wife. Don't worry. I'll take care of the reservation. Can't wait. And you're right. We don't need to make long-term plans and set this up as a recurring event. The more open and spontaneous we are, the more in the flow we'll become. I feel it. To me, that's exciting too. How can we maintain that connection to each other?

Nancy: I'm excited too! We both have to make an effort to really invest in having a deep connection with each other. If we can get to a level of sensuality and intimacy like that, I feel we can enjoy each other deeply.

I'm looking forward to having more emotional and physical intimacy with you.

Fred: Absolutely. I'm so happy that I brought this up. It's been bothering me for a while. We've come up with a solution we both feel excited about. Let's do this together.

Did you see how Fred started off with an I-Feel Statement and then made his I-Need Statement? Did you notice how Nancy became defensive at first but then, beautifully, shifted her communication into I-Feel statements and asked an Open-Ended Curious Question to see where Fred was? Connecting with Nancy's sensitivity, Fred leveled with an Aikido Move. He accepted his fault—his narrow focus on his needs only—and asked her an Open-Ended Curious Question to learn more about where she was coming from.

Did you catch how well Fred applied Holding Space with Attentive Listening, where Nancy felt comfortable opening up about her needs? As she kept expressing her thoughts about how they could create an intimate connection, the flow of the conversation turned into a harmonious, engaged interaction.

After they understood each other's point of view, they could work together toward a common goal that would satisfy most of each other's needs. Of course, both had to agree to a level of compromise, but in the end, you could tell how curious they were about how this new mutually agreed upon solution would transform their relationship.

How did you feel when you were reading this dialogue? Could you put yourself in their shoes and feel confident applying some of these strategies in your daily interactions?

Well, I'm not sure yet. These are very advanced strategies. Can you share a few more examples so I can understand them better?

Of course. Here are three scenarios for you. Try to be in the shoes of the individual you most relate to. See if you could mimic their approach. When experimenting with the 7 Communication Strategies, let your experiences guide you in the right direction. Learning from every mistake and using that knowledge to adjust your next Communication Strategy will enhance your engagement, deepen your connection, and tremendously improve your relationship.

Scenario One

The Trigger: Another weekend is approaching, and Diane wants to go out and have a date night with her husband, Jeff, to rekindle their connection, which has been deteriorating lately. She has been asking Jeff to devise a plan for a special night. They've been married for five years and have come down from the initial high of their relationship, especially during the last two years after they had their first child, Zach. Diane has started worrying about whether their relationship could endure for the long haul. Still, she decides to push through and see if Jeff will turn around and become the warm, emotional, affectionate guy she fell in love with early on in their relationship. Diane's mom looks forward to babysitting, especially if Diane and Jeff want to spend time alone. But now, it's Thursday. Jeff won't tell her anything about their weekend plans, even though she mentioned going to the city Saturday night.

Emotions: Diane is anxious because she doesn't know if Jeff will come through this time and show his love to her. He's often aloof, distant, and seems checked out. Maybe that's why she also gets angry with him. How many times does she need to tell him that she wants to be closer to him and spend quality time together? She finds trying to communicate with Jeff extremely frustrating and sad. Why can't they work things out?

Thoughts: Diane thinks Jeff doesn't care about her or their relationship. He's always been good at doing his own thing, but when it comes to their relationship, he seems passive and distant. Deep down, Diane believes Jeff has lost interest in her, doesn't value her as much, and doesn't want to spend time with her. She wonders if he may not find her attractive enough to be around anymore.

Feelings: Along with those thoughts of not being valued and not being good enough for her husband, Diane feels rejected and dismissed. She feels like her needs are constantly ignored, but she doesn't feel worthy of speaking up to ask that they be met. She stays in the relationship for their child and puts up with Jeff's nonchalant, uninterested attitude, but she feels devalued and unimportant and has considered packing her bags and leaving.

Repressed Fears: These feelings have been common throughout Diane's life. She remembers her college boyfriend doing the same thing. He preferred to stay in the dormitory and play video games rather than go out with her to a restaurant and have a good time on the weekend. Maybe that's when she developed these repressed fears of not being good enough, not being worthy of care, and not being valued. She had never thought about this before, but lately, she has also started feeling a fear of being boring. She's afraid that if it's true that she's not an interesting person and Jeff leaves her, she'll be lonely for the rest of her life.

Origins: When reflecting on her need to spend more time with Jeff, in addition to the memories of her boyfriend from college, Diane also remembers having a big fallout with two close girlfriends she had in high school. She used to hang out with them almost every day and frequently gathered at each other's houses. They were really close and tried to do everything together. Then, a new girl came to their class at the beginning of ninth grade, and just like that, both of her friends stopped talking to Diane. Her friends abandoned her and started hanging out with the new girl. It was devastating. One day, she had two best friends; the next day, they were gone. It was shocking for her to lose that deep connection and her clan. She remembers spending September and October crying in her room for hours.

Old Reaction: Well, surprise, surprise! Jeff didn't come through, and Diane has another disappointing, uneventful weekend of chores and family routines. Diane is pissed off. Usually, she gets through the weekend and then calls her friend on Monday morning to complain about her husband's lack of interest in her and their relationship. She questions whether Jeff is right for her and reminisces about how great everything was with him in the beginning, but now he's distant and cold. She also says that she wishes her husband was a different person or at least the person she married five years ago.

New Response: Now that Diane is taking this course on emotional mastery, she challenges herself to try Doing the Opposite. What if she opens up to Jeff and tells him what she's feeling to see if she can help get anything going? She decides to skip her usual call with her friend on Monday morning and then asks Jeff if he's available Tuesday night for a quick bite at the local bistro. On Tuesday night, they sit down at their favorite spot in the restaurant, Jeff a little warily and Diane with her game face on. Without wasting time, she jumps right in,

"Jeff, honey, for the last couple of months, I've been asking to go out and spend time with you. I've been pretty vocal about my desire. Did we do it? No, we didn't. I feel rejected. I don't know how else to say it. What should I do to go on a date with you? I feel dismissed and ignored, and to be honest, this makes me feel unattractive, not interesting, and not valued. I feel like I'm nobody."

To her surprise, Jeff responds unapologetically and with a calm voice. "I've been thinking about that also, Diane. But what I realized is that whenever I initiate a date night, make a reservation at a restaurant, or get tickets for a show, you complain about everything—the food, traffic to the city, how rude people are, how late we stay, and you're worried about how our son is doing. It's not fun for me. So I stopped initiating anything."

Diane feels shocked. Is Jeff blaming her for them not going out? Then, she pauses to observe and welcome whatever feelings arise in her body. After grounding her emotions, she replies calmly, "I hear you. Maybe you can tell me more about how you felt on those nights. I didn't realize how much I complained. Is that a reason not to go out again? I didn't realize how my complaints affected you."

Jeff tells her more about what he thought during those nights, and Diane holds space for Jeff and listens to him reflect on her attitude. Finally, Diane does one more Aikido Move, saying, "Okay, I agree with you, honey. I guess I was a handful and too critical, which killed the buzz. I'm now aware of it." She immediately follows up with the I-Need and Collaborative We Strategies, saying, "It's important for me to spend quality time with you, Jeff. I need closeness and connection to feel valued and accepted. It seems like we both want the same thing. How can we get past this and try again? What do you think about me making some arrangements in the city for the upcoming weekend?" Jeff nods, smiling, and reaches out for a warm, close hug. They now feel ready to add more spark to their relationship.

Scenario Two

The Trigger: Alison drops her friend Jackie off at the airport and then doesn't hear from her for a few weeks. She wonders if she said something in the car that offended her friend. Even though she doesn't feel Jackie is a good friend, Alison always says yes for some reason whenever Jackie calls her to ask a favor. The morning Alison took Jackie to the airport was one of those beautiful days in the San Francisco Bay Area, and Alison had originally planned on going to the beach. Instead, she ended up in the car with Jackie, feeling like she needed to walk on eggshells to avoid saying something wrong.

Alison blames Jackie for being a distant friend and not connecting with her. Still, Alison also realizes that she didn't say no to Jackie, even though she knew her friend was just using her generosity to save a few bucks on Uber.

Emotions: Alison is furious at her friend. She's also frustrated with herself for not setting firm boundaries. She knows why she struggles with that, though. She always feels anxious about losing her friend. She doesn't want to break ties with Jackie, but it's getting to a point where Alison constantly feels triggered by her. Her resentment makes her not want to talk to Jackie again. But part of her also wants to continue the friendship.

Thoughts: Alison blames Jackie for not valuing the time and friendship Alison offers. Alison also thinks Jackie is manipulative and always has a hidden agenda. Jackie uses everyone, not just Alison, for her benefit, and Alison has never once heard Jackie mention that she appreciates the help she gets from Alison.

Feelings: Alison feels used, taken for granted, not valued, unappreciated, and worthless.

Repressed Fears: Fear of not being valued, fear of being nobody, not being special, always being at the service of others, and fear of being lonely.

Origins: On the way back from the airport, Alison has time to reflect on why she keeps giving up her life for others and making them a priority. Why does she so desperately need to meet others' expectations? She then realizes that when she was growing up, her parents were both emotionally unavailable and quite distant. As a family, they didn't talk much at home. Everyone knew what they were supposed to do and did it without question. She sensed early on, without her parents telling her anything, what she needed to do to meet their expectations. But whenever she did what was expected of her, her parents didn't give feedback, so Alison never understood or had a sense of whether she was doing okay or not.

This lack of communication made her try to do more for her parents, and this behavior of pleasing them, begging for approval, and craving positive feedback became her destructive drama cycle. She is a people pleaser, and Jackie intimidates her. Alison feels less than and thinks Jackie is better than her, a cool, powerful person to please. As Alison continues reverse engineering her feelings and repressed fears, she realizes that she keeps trying to meet Jackie's needs and expectations, hoping that one day, Jackie will approve of her, provide positive feedback, and maybe accept her into her friends' circles.

Old Response: Alison has decided to break from her friendship with Jackie a million times before but has never dared to follow through. She sweeps her frustrations under the rug and stays quiet when her text messages to Jackie are not answered in a timely fashion. Eventually, things cool off, and Alison gets a new text message from Alison. Out of the blue, she's inviting Alison to a get-together with friends that evening. She wants to know if she'll be there and be able to pick up Jackie's clothes from the dry cleaner on the way. Without hesitation, Alison says yes and feels good about being invited. Every time she gives in, her resentment toward Jackie grows. It's not like she hasn't tried. A few times in the past, she raised her voice with anger and resentment, but it didn't have much effect on the outcome. Jackie has continued to ignore Alison until she needs something.

New Response: After the trip to the airport, Alison decides to try Doing the Opposite and talk to Jackie about how she's feeling about the whole situation. She hopes that everything goes well and no conflict arises from this. Alison doesn't want to hurt Jackie; she would feel guilty doing that. On Thursday night, she decides to call Jackie, knowing she'll have just returned from her trip.

Surprisingly, Jackie answers Alison's call. "Hey, what's up?"

Alison gathers her strength, applies everything she knows about the Power Method, takes a big inhale, exhales every tension in her body through the bottoms of her feet, and starts talking. "Hey, Jackie, not much. I was just calling you to say that it didn't feel cool that I went out of my way to drop you off at the airport last week and never heard back when I texted and asked you to share some of your pictures from your trip to Aruba." Alison stops talking. An awkward silence ensues. She panics that it may be too much to dump on Jackie. After all, Jackie just got back from a week-long vacation. Then Jackie replies nonchalantly, "I was too busy. I didn't see your texts."

Alison gets confused. Now, what does she do? All her remarks have fallen short. She collects herself and manages to apply the Open-Ended Curious Question and asks, "Well, I'm curious what you would have done if I hadn't dropped you off at the airport and hadn't picked you up yesterday after I'd waited for an hour because you forgot to text me that your flight got delayed."

Jackie says, "I would have called an Uber. I thought you wanted to hang out with me. That's why I called you." Alison starts to get angry and becomes more anxious about communicating with Jackie about how upset she is about the situation. She grounds herself and hesitantly begins to talk again. "Well, yes, you're right; I want to hang out with you because I want to be your friend. But recently, I realized that it's a one-way friendship, even if we could call it friendship. I feel dismissed, ignored, and devalued. What should I do to make this friendship work?"

Jackie takes her time and then almost whispers her reply. "You can't do much, Alison. I don't think we're compatible. You pressure me too much to do this or to do that. Yes, I saw your texts about the pictures. Why would I take a moment in my day to take pictures and send them to you? If you want pictures, go on vacation and take your own. I'm sick and tired of you pestering me with constant requests and demands."

Alison is shocked by the honesty of Jackie's comments but finds a few seconds to inhale and exhale the charge and replies, "Okay, I understand. Yes, I can see my role in it. I guess I wanted to be your friend so much that I requested those pictures so that I could feel connected with you. I now realize how annoying that could be. I need to feel the closeness in friendships. Friendships are not ad hoc 'take me to the airport' calls. I was reflecting on what we could do to improve our interactions, but I guess there's not much to discuss here. Wishing you all the best! Bye!"

Alison hangs up the phone when she hears Jackie's "Bye!" on the other end and sits back on her sofa, crying uncontrollably. Her body shakes as if she's shedding layers of repressed fears from the past of feeling devalued, less than, and worthless. The conversation prompts her to face her fears with more courage, and she decides to take her life back. A few weeks later, she books a solo trip to Paris.

Scenario Three

The Trigger: Linda's son, nineteen-year-old Kevin, has a drinking problem. She doesn't know how to deal with her son and his situation. She has tried to control his drinking by limiting his outings with his friends, but now that he's about to leave their home in Los Angeles and go to college in Boston, she's extremely worried that his partying will get out of control and affect his grades and his future. She wants to fly with him to get him settled in his dorm in Boston, but Kevin thinks it's not cool to have his mom come along and pushes back on her accompanying him on this trip.

Emotions: Linda is anxious and worried about her son's life out of town. She's also frustrated that she can't get her son to agree to her joining him for the first couple of weeks of his life in Boston.

Feelings: Linda feels disrespected, hopeless, powerless, disregarded, and dismissed. Now that she will be an empty nester, she also feels lonely and purposeless as her son moves out of the home. Who knows when they'll get to spend time together again?

Repressed Fears: Linda realizes that she fears abandonment, being left behind, and loneliness. Even though her feelings are all over the place, she notices that she's actually sad because she fears being abandoned by her son.

Origins: As Linda is sitting in Conscious Discomfort of her pain and what she needs to face in a few months when Kevin departs, she comes to a huge realization that her dad had left home for two years after he got assigned to a work project in Switzerland when she was fourteen years old. Soon after he came back, her parents decided to get divorced, and her relationship with her dad was never the same. He had been loving toward her before the separation, but afterward, for some reason, he put a lot of emotional distance between them. Linda also didn't get along with her mom, so it was hard to be left with her after the divorce. Linda now understands why she's so angry at Kevin when he goes out with his friends, drinks until after midnight, and hardly spends time with her. She realizes that she projects her original anger toward her dad and feelings of abandonment onto Kevin, who is already checked out and doesn't want to be around Linda.

Old Reaction: Linda has kept putting limitations on Kevin's behavior. She tries to control alcohol purchases that are brought home.

She occasionally yells at him for spending all his time in his room, talking to his friends, watching baseball, or playing video games. She complains to her husband about Kevin's actions, but her husband doesn't see any problems, saying, "Leave him alone. He's young. He needs space. I was like him; look, nothing's wrong with my life. I have a great family, a great job, and a great house. He'll be okay. Let him live his life." These conversations with her husband always lead to drama, and they start arguing as she tries to convince her husband to be more watchful over their son.

New Response: A few weeks before Kevin leaves for Boston, Linda knocks on the door of his room and interrupts his video game, asking for a minute to chat. Surprised and very annoyed, Kevin unwillingly invites her in. Linda says, "Kev, I know I've been on your case since you were little. I've always wanted you to be a great kid—the way I see you in my eyes. We don't always get along, but recently, I've felt our connection is broken."

Kevin interrupts Linda right there, as he starts to get uncomfortable with where the conversation is going, and says, "Nothing's wrong, Mom, we're cool. I'll be out of here in a few weeks, and I won't be bothering you anymore."

Linda feels curious about what she hears. She asks, "What do you mean by bothering me? You're not bothering me."

Kevin replies casually, "I know I'm not the kid you want me to be. I'm a disappointment to you."

Linda immediately holds space for him as Kevin elaborates, "I'm very embarrassed about my drinking problem. You see, I even call it a problem now. But sincerely, I don't know what to do about it."

After her son stops talking, Linda replies, "First of all, yes, I'm sensitive. That's for sure. And I see you are, too. And nothing's wrong with that. We're heart people. I care for you. I've been so reactive to you because I'm afraid of having distance between us.

But the more I want us to be closer, the farther you go."

Kevin jumps in, saying, "But Mom! You're so controlling. You're in my business all the time."

Linda holds more space as he makes this comment. When it's her turn to respond, she admits, "Yes, you're right. I've been a very controlling mom. I didn't realize what I was doing wasn't about your actions but came from my fear of losing you. You're my only child. You're my precious baby. I know it's not fair to you, and I probably suffocated you with my interventions. Now I see everything clearly. I'm so happy that you're going to Boston. You're a fine man now. Go and do your thing. I trust you will make good judgments. It's hard to admit that you don't need me anymore, but I'm so proud of who you are and the future you will create."

After that, Kevin gets up from his chair and hugs his mom tightly. They stay in each other's arms for several minutes, which feels like an eternity to both, as they realize how much warm and deep connection they crave from each other. While hugging, Linda softly tells Kevin, "I'd love to stay in touch, not as a controlling mother, but maybe like a loving mother. How can we work together to accomplish that? What do we do to stay connected while you're gone?"

Kevin separates himself from Linda for a moment and, with a calm, understanding voice, says, "I'm not planning to abandon you, Mom. How about we play it by ear and be spontaneous about our interactions? Let's not make scheduled calls but call each other periodically. How would that work for you?"

Linda realizes right then that Kevin has grown up and is ready to start his own life.

JOURNAL ENTRY FOR WEEK FOUR

For the next seven days, make a journal entry at the end of each day to capture the most intense trigger event that occurred. Do this review by answering the following questions:

1. What was the trigger event?
2. What emotions did you experience?
3. What thoughts did you have?
4. What were your feelings?
5. Can you identify your repressed fears?
6. What are their origins?
7. What physical sensations did you experience?
8. What is your typical reaction?
9. What will be your new Communication Strategy?

DAILY CHECKLIST FOR WEEK FOUR

1. Have you practiced the following Power Steps?

    - Pause to notice your emotions
    - Observe your thoughts
    - Welcome the physical sensations
    - Earth the emotional charge

2. Have you practiced the following Power Techniques?

    - Square Breathing
    - Self-Observation Meditation
    - 3-by-3 Breath
    - Grounding

3. Have you practiced the following Power Tools?

    - I'm {the emotion}
    - What If—So What
    - Conscious Discomfort
    - Exhaling Out of the Feet

4. Have you used any of the following Communication Strategies?

   - Doing the Opposite
   - Using I-Feel Statements
   - Asking Open-Ended Curious Questions
   - Holding Space with Attentive Listening
   - Leveling with an Aikido Move
   - Using I-Need Statements
   - Asking Collaborative We Questions

CHAPTER SIX

FROM LEARNING TO LIVING

Making Emotional Mastery Second Nature

You're attending Thanksgiving dinner at your beloved Auntie's house. She loves cooking for the family. It's another festive gathering with about twenty family members ready to have a great meal together. It starts off very well. You love catching up with your cousins. Suddenly, as the dinner is about to be served, your uncle makes an off comment and asks how your diet is going. You notice he's a little tipsy, yet you're taken aback by his question.

Right at that moment, you look for your usual anger. But tonight, you find yourself getting irritated instead of angry. The intensity is simply not there. You're taking your uncle's comments in stride. It's shocking to you. Such offensive, inconsiderate comments would have usually set you off. As a matter of fact, you left last year's Thanksgiving dinner early because your uncle, again, commented on how many diets you had done thus far.

Tonight, you pause naturally. Then, you observe your thoughts and feelings. Yes, you're irritated. But you now know why. It comes from your insecurity about your body and your weight. And one thing that you didn't want to happen is happening now: being put down in front of the family. You've written so many times in your Daily Review Journal. So you're ready for this moment. You immediately do a quick 3-by-3 Breath, ground your energy by earthing your irritation into the floor, and respond calmly, "Uncle Tom, I feel put down! How is it that every year, I get a question about my diet? What exactly would you like to know?"

Thirty people suddenly stop talking. The five-second silence in Auntie's dining room feels like five hours. All eyes are on Uncle Tom. He's speechless. He doesn't know how to respond. His eyes look down, and he murmurs, "I'm sorry. I didn't mean to pick on you." Everyone breathes a sigh of relief. You can see a little smile on everybody's faces as if they approve of your standing up for yourself. It's like a little personal victory in the middle of a Thanksgiving dinner that you'll never forget. The night goes on with you feeling more comfortable and moving freely in your body.

How does this sound for progress? You've come so far in your emotional mastery training. You've learned how to regulate your emotional reactions and respond to adversaries with a calm, grounded, and centered presence. And now you're getting ready to be able to walk on the path to happiness alone with more self-awareness, self-knowledge, and wisdom.

Emotional mastery is more than just a method; it's a life skill. It is a journey. And as such, your abilities and capacity to execute mastery will become more potent over time. With more practice, the Power Method and its Communication Strategies will become second nature to you. When you reach such heights, you'll become more conscious of your fight-or-flight defense mechanisms. During trigger events, more and more, you'll be able to see that mental space and choose your responses to people more consciously.

Having this awareness shifts the power and control of your life into your hands rather than being lost in your unconscious reactions to people. Let's see how you can keep your training on track and make sure emotional mastery becomes a core part of who you are and how you live your life. I'm curious to see how far you can take this journey.

Certainly, I've been having interesting breakthroughs in my interactions with others. But I still don't know how to measure my progress. How do I know where I'm on my path?

Of course, you'd like to know the coordinates of your location, how far you've come, and whether you're on track to achieve emotional mastery.

Working with over six thousand clients over the last fifteen years, I've seen the following three signs confirming your progress on the path to happiness. By the way, at this point, if you have done your homework and used the tools and techniques you've learned, I expect you to have already experienced these positive shifts in your life. You're about to switch from learning to living the eternal gifts of emotional mastery.

FIRST SIGN OF PROGRESS: TRIGGERS BECOME LESS INTENSE

When you practice pause, you achieve an expanded mental space; in that space, you observe your thoughts more calmly and attentively. They pass through your mind's eye in slow motion. You realize you can still interact with others while you observe your thoughts. When you get to that stage, one day, out of nowhere, you realize some of the triggers that used to bother you don't have as strong of a hold as before.

Many of my clients simply can't believe when this phenomenon happens. In the beginning, they doubt its sustainability. They usually think it's a one-off, random occurrence. I have stopped trying to convince them that it's the result of their training and deep personal work and let them doubt their progress. But sooner or later, they realize that triggers are naturally loosening their stranglehold over their emotional reactions and lessening the negative impact on their mental and emotional states.

When (and not if) that happens to you, please take a moment to celebrate. You're on the path, on your way to emotional mastery.

SECOND SIGN OF PROGRESS: TRIGGERS BECOME LESS FREQUENT

Before, you had strong, intense, repressed fears, right? You were stuck in destructive drama cycles. You had to deal with complex and challenging people who constantly triggered you. When you process and release your repressed fears, they magically loosen their grip on you.

This shift occurs mainly because you can now stand up for yourself and express your feelings with clear and powerful Communication Strategies. You can do that because you have received the special message that triggers carry for you: "Learn about your repressed fears, process them, and then release them to claim your power!"

Once you do this gratifying personal work, the triggers back off as if they have accomplished their mission and you have established healthy boundaries with those around you. Whether or not you have experienced this phenomenon, I invite you to experiment with the 7 Communication Strategies more diligently and witness what happens over time.

After three to four months of daily practice of the Power Method, you notice that the fruitless arguments, damaging conflicts, endless back-and-forths, and personal jabs—whether they're with your spouse, kids, colleagues, or friends—are not as frequent as they were before. When you realize how a period of time has passed with no apparent drama, you may be surprised by how others are no longer combative, critical, or judgmental but more accommodating and in a harmonious flow in your interactions.

Of course, this sign of progress can only be achieved by doing your personal work diligently, consistently, and with genuine commitment. When you do your part first, others respond to you with sincerity. When you change how you interact with them, you can rightfully expect a positive shift in others, and you receive it. When you do, the world is yours. Your life opens up with all sorts of possibilities and opportunities. All you have to do then is embrace life fully on the path to happiness.

THIRD SIGN OF PROGRESS: RECOVERY FROM TRIGGERS IS QUICKER

This sign is the easiest to spot because the shift is so drastic. Remember those days when a trigger event happened and lingered in your mind for hours, if not days or weeks? During those moments when you had to deal with difficult and challenging people, your body and mind were completely tense with constant thoughts about them.

Even when you put your head on your pillow at night, you conspired about what you could have done differently in those triggers, how you could have had a better comeback, or even done something to hurt them so that they understood what they did to you. With those intense thoughts in your mind, you spent a lot of sleepless nights and didn't have the energy to enjoy your days.

I hope those days and nights slowly come to an end for you. Let's face it. You had those experiences because you didn't have the foundation to respond to others appropriately. You didn't have healthy boundaries. But now you do. Your emotional regulation baseline is higher than it's ever been before. You don't have to wait until night-time to conspire how to get revenge. You can respond to people in the moment and stand up for yourself. When you do, you stay somewhat undisturbed whenever you get triggered. As a result, your tumble into emotional despair is shorter, and the recovery time is faster than before.

To measure this phenomenon, simply observe how many hours or days you occupy your mind with a trigger event. How long do you stay emotionally out of balance? How long does it take for you to shake a trigger off? Pay attention to the residual effects of your triggers. The moment you realize that you recover from triggers in far less time than you used to is another reason to celebrate your progress.

I find it fascinating how you can change your life by simply changing your emotional reactions. When you experience these signs and confirmations of your progress that you're on the path to happiness, pat yourself on the back. You deserve all the credit for the personal work you've done so far. If the shift seems few and far between, double down on your practices of Power Steps, Tools, and Techniques, and lean in more to have a better execution of your Communication Strategies. The path to happiness is laid out in front of you. You just need to keep practicing emotional mastery.

When I'm using these strategies, sometimes the other person doesn't let it go and keeps coming back at me. I end up getting emotionally charged and want to counter-argue. How do I keep my composure and not get involved?

Remember that you will encounter waves of resistance any time you use a new Communication Strategy. It's only natural. Your awareness is different from that of others. Think about this phenomenon as though two people speak French, but their levels of language proficiency are different. A fluent speaker says, "I feel this and that," and the less fluent person replies, "Huh? I don't understand. Can you speak slowly?"

When such dissonance exists between two people, it's likely to cause a rift in their interactions. When that happens, your job, as a student of emotional mastery, is not to react emotionally to the sudden break in the communication but to be curious enough to investigate what's happening.

Whether you choose to argue with or run away from people who can't accept your new way of communicating, you'll eventually end up having another destructive drama cycle with them or others sometime later. Therefore, try to deal with the situation right there and then. After all, every trigger has a message. It's an invitation to look inward. Use every opportunity to discover your subconscious programming that instigates your emotional reactions.

Once you know that you can't really win an argument, overpower others, or run away from anything or anyone, you realize that the only way to avoid these situations is to work on yourself. When you face your vulnerability and process your repressed fears, your interactions with those who trigger you become smoother.

But coming back to your question, what if someone resists hearing you out when you're putting your feelings into I-Feel Statements? What if they refuse to answer your Open-Ended Curious Questions? What if they keep defending their point of view? What is the message when they trigger you even more with their attitude? Can you pause? Can you observe your thoughts? Can you apply your 3-by-3 Breath? Can you sit in Conscious Discomfort? Can you ground that emotional charge? Can you try a Communication Strategy? And then, yet again, can you question your vulnerability? What is your attachment? What is at stake? What repressed fear do they provoke?

Maybe start from the beginning and use Doing the Opposite

to them by walking away from an argument you really care about winning. Then, consciously connect with the discomfort of not challenging the other person as you used to. Identify your repressed fears and attachments to the outcome and see if you can dig deeper into their origins to understand your current emotional reactions to a trigger event.

I'm afraid that's the work, my friend. And I'm sure you intuitively sense how the rewards of a drama-free life can far outweigh the little bit of extra effort you need to put in against those waves of resistance. Keep coming back to the Grounding technique to anchor yourself whenever you face such situations. All that being said, the best method for dealing with escalating arguments and stopping them abruptly is the Aikido Move. Once you establish your position with that, you can make I-Need Statements to open the doors for Collaborative We Questions to drive the conversation toward beneficial solutions and lead the interaction toward deeper connections.

When using these advanced techniques, be careful of your attachments to a specific outcome and your expectations of others. If you maintain a slight attachment or expectation, you may not be able to withstand the waves of resistance, and you'll end up getting sucked into another endless argument with the other person. Stay grounded. If it seems almost impossible to get out of that loop, challenge your thoughts with the "What If—So What" Question and see if it will save you from falling further into your subconscious fight-or-flight defense mechanisms. Keep this technique as a secret weapon in your pocket and use it as much as possible. It's a lifesaver.

When you repeat the steps of the Power Method and keep trying all 7 Communication Strategies for almost every trigger event, before you know it, you realize the waves of resistance are no longer the giant mavericks of world surf competitions but the soft ripples of the Mediterranean Sea.

Most of the time, you've talked about external triggers. How about my own thoughts? What if my negative self-talk triggers me? What do I do then?

A trigger is a trigger. Wouldn't you agree? Your thoughts and negative self-talk can act as triggers, eliciting intense emotional reactions in you. But do you think the process of handling them will be different than any external trigger? Certainly not. You still need to go through each step of the Power Method, one by one, and treat your thoughts as usual triggers.

For example, can you pause when those negative thoughts invade your mind? Can you objectively and neutrally observe them as if they are the clouds going by? Can you unhook from the negative thoughts, create mental space by pausing, and then challenge them with "What If— So What" Questions?

More importantly, can you go deep enough to discover the feelings and repressed fears that cause your thoughts and emotions to flare up, and then consciously welcome those negative, self-deprecating thoughts through Conscious Discomfort and accept them with an Aikido Move by understanding where they may have come from originally?

You can follow this protocol the same way you do your Self-Observation Meditation practice. Simply observe your negative self-talk by staying as detached and observant as possible without getting hooked on negative stories, worries, and concerns as the product of your mind. Your success in applying these strategies comes down to how well you manage your attention, for which you've been consistently training.

Maybe this shortcut works for you: Experiment with pausing vigorously whenever you catch yourself lost in negative self-talk. Then, use the Grounding technique to return to the present moment. Play around with Doing the Opposite strategies and find the best one that works against your own self-deprecating thoughts. Finally, reflect on them every night during your Daily Review and make adjustments the following day.

Can you recap the situation about the date night incident you shared at the beginning to showcase emotional mastery and how you could have used all 7 Communication Strategies if it happened today?

Sure, let's review that situation one more time. First, my wife tells me to slow down because I'm driving too close to the car in front of us. Let's see how the conversation develops when I use the 5-Step Power Method and all the Communication Strategies after I emotionally react to her.

First, when I hear my wife's suggestion to slow down, I feel an intense frustration. I pause to notice it. I immediately observe my thoughts: *Oh, not again; she's controlling me!* I can't control my frustration, and I raise my voice. "No, we're not driving too close. See, there's plenty of space!"

She is visibly taken aback. On top of her anxiety about my reckless driving, she feels dismissed and unheard. She repeats more assertively, "You need to give more space. I don't feel safe!"

Meanwhile, I find the emotional charge in my stomach, which has escalated from frustration to anger. I immediately apply the 3-by-3 Breath while I listen to my wife repeat her statement to change my behavior. The emotional charge is still so tense that I can't feel the bottoms of my feet yet.

I object again with an aggressive question, which is not curious but sounds more like a statement, "Why do you keep controlling me?" As soon as I say it, I want to take it away. I realize it's going to make this conversation go downhill very quickly. I'm in shock that I'm in this destructive drama cycle again. In that desperate moment,

I find my ground through the bottoms of my feet and exhale fully to shift the energy.

Following that adjustment, I brake and back off considerably to maintain a reasonably safe distance between our car and the one in front of us before I say anything else. The Doing the Opposite strategy seems to have worked, as I can see the relief on my wife's face. To turn the conversation around, I need to apply the Aikido Move to level with her.

Then I reply, "You are right. We are too close. I got defensive. I was distracted by the excitement of going out on a date tonight and was rushing a little bit. It's been a long time, and I couldn't wait."

My wife, seemingly more relaxed, says, "Thank you for slowing down. I feel more comfortable now, and I'll enjoy our ride to the restaurant. I can't wait either! It's going to be fun. We don't need to rush. We have plenty of time."

Using a calm tone, I reply, "I also want to share something with you. For some reason, I felt controlled and got angry when I heard you question my driving."

This is a not-so-well-executed I-Feel Statement; I used a you-statement when I shared it. However, the tone makes a difference. Let's see if she'll get triggered and blame me for driving too fast. If she does, that means my tone was defensive. If she doesn't react, I struck an appropriately neutral, nondefensive tone of voice.

My wife audibly inhales and exhales, almost rolling her eyes, and responds with some annoyance – I have triggered her with my you-statement. "I wasn't questioning your driving. I was getting anxious because you weren't paying attention to the car in front of us, and it was slowing down. You know how important it is for me to feel safe on the road."

Her response shows that I must have used a defensive tone and maybe even sounded like I was explaining my position. As a result, she started to use you-statements to confirm her perspective and clear up any doubt that she was blaming me. You can see how if I take her words personally, this could go into an unproductive "he said, she said" back-and-forth. I need to apply all five steps of the Power Method at this point.

After some quick introspection, I reply, "Okay, I understand where you're coming from, and I know the car accident you experienced years ago still takes an emotional toll on you. That's why I slowed down after you pointed out we were too close. I still feel controlled, though. I'd like to process that. Maybe it's because when I was growing up, I felt judged, and people were overly critical of me whenever I did something wrong." I'm using a series of I-Feel Statements to neutralize the energy between us. This time, I avoid using you-statements, except for matter-of-factly referring to an incident we both know about.

After I say this, my wife gets curious and says, "Thank you for understanding. I really appreciate you sharing information about your upbringing with me. Would you tell me more about how you felt when I told you to slow down?" She's asking an Open-Ended Curious Question using "how," along with an encouraging close-ended question (would you like), which sounds like an invitation for me to open up so that she can practice Holding Space with Attentive Listening.

Now that I feel the space my wife is creating, I am more relaxed and start sharing my deeper thoughts. "Yes, this anger came up from deep down, and I felt trapped. I know it's a small comment, and you didn't judge me. I'm extremely calm now and know exactly where you're coming from. You know it happens sometimes. One comment, one gesture, one attitude, and I go right back to my childhood. I have memories of my mom and dad fighting in the car over small things while we were driving on family outings. There was always conflict. And I was so angry at them for having problems during a supposedly happy family time. I guess the comment took me back. What did your family do in times of conflict?"

Again, note that I've used I-Feel Statements all the way. Notice how it was a pure monologue, sharing my thoughts and feelings and how my past affected my emotional reactions. After opening up with these statements, I finish with an Open-Ended Curious question to bring her into the conversation, get to know her more intimately, and inquire about her past.

With a contemplative voice, my wife says, "My parents used to fight a lot too. They would disagree on everything—about where to go, where to eat, and where to park whenever we went camping on the weekends. It was a nightmare, and I also hated every moment. How interesting! You and I had similar experiences, but we react to things differently."

I am curious about my wife's past. She has more to say, and I'd like to learn more about her. I prepare to hold space for her and encourage her to talk about her past. "Oh, really? Tell me more about these camping trips. I didn't know you guys did that. How old were you then? Did you enjoy them? How did you deal with your family drama then?"

As you can tell, I'm asking a lot of Open-Ended Curious Questions to invite her to talk. I maintain my grounded state and Hold Space with Attentive Listening to open the energy in our interaction so that she feels more comfortable speaking and sharing her intimate thoughts, feelings, and past experiences.

My wife then shares with me the feelings and experiences she had during her childhood right up until we arrive at the restaurant. Dinner goes very well. Afterward, while waiting for our dessert, I open up the topic again to have full closure. "You know, my love, it was not nice of me to raise my voice back in the car. I should have remembered how important it is for you to feel safe when driving on the highway. I got too defensive. I projected everything from my past onto you and treated you as if you were my controlling parents. How hilarious! Even though you control me sometimes, you're not even close to them. You can't beat them. And I should stop projecting all of that onto you."

Now, I make this statement with a smile. I admit my part in the conflict when I level with an Aikido Move. After grounding my energy, especially after a few hours of the incident and a beautiful dinner in between, I can now clearly see what I did, how I reacted, and why I reacted that way. In a sense, this last statement serves as a closure of the earlier conflict. It resets the energy in the connection and makes it deeper for future interactions.

My wife warmly smiles at me and assures me that everything is okay. She says she's not dwelling on it.

That was another day in our ordinary life.

JOURNAL ENTRY FOR WEEK FIVE

For the next seven days, make a journal entry at the end of each day to capture the most intense trigger event that occurred. Do this review by answering the following questions:

1. What was the trigger event?
2. What emotions did you experience?
3. What thoughts did you have?
4. What were your feelings?
5. Can you identify your repressed fears?
6. What are their origins?
7. What physical sensations did you experience?
8. What is your typical reaction?
9. What will be your new Communication Strategy?

DAILY CHECKLIST FOR WEEK FIVE

1. Have you experienced any of the following three signs of progress?

   - Are triggers less intense?

   - Are triggers less frequent?

   - Is your recovery from triggers quicker?

If your answer is no to all three questions, then please go back and start from week one, paying attention to practicing the Power Techniques more diligently and consistently.

After all, without the training, it's difficult to overcome your subconscious programming. Without properly processing your repressed fears, you lose motivation to achieve emotional mastery. Only through applying the 5-Step Power Method and its Communication Strategies can you get back on track and find your footing on the path to true happiness.

CONCLUSION

Rising Above Drama

Walking the Path Toward Realizing True Happiness

As you reach the end of your emotional mastery training, let's take a moment to reflect on the key insights we've explored together. You've started this journey questioning what has plagued your relationships and made you unhappy. You soon realized that it is the drama you experience in your relationships, day in and day out. Before practicing emotional mastery, you thought others created the drama. But, as you've explored your experiences more deeply, you've realized that you simply give your power away to others and blame them for taking it.

As you've learned how to regulate your intense emotions, improve your communication, and create better interactions, you've noticed that it's actually in your hands to take control of your subconscious and be in charge of your automatic, fight-or-flight defense mechanisms. By practicing the Power Tools and Techniques, you've slowly equipped yourself to navigate life's emotional ups and downs more easily and assertively.

Your commitment to developing emotional mastery is a profound step toward personal growth. Think back to where you started and how far you've come. You now have a deeper understanding of yourself and those around you, fostering presence, empathy, and resilience. This journey has been about more than just learning techniques; it's been about transforming your perspective on how relationships work and, more importantly, how to bring about the happiness everyone desires.

This new approach is a game changer. You no longer expect others to behave in a certain way to make you happy. Can you believe you no longer need to rely on them for happiness? You now know that creating deeper connections is in your hands. To that extent, you've learned some powerful reverse engineering tools that help you dive deep below the surface, beneath your emotions, to see how your repressed fears create your fight-or-flight defense mechanisms. You've finally realized how those automatic reactions are the culprits that take away the happiness you crave.

For that reason, and for that reason alone, you can't expect someone else to make you happy. And the reverse is also true: you can't expect someone else to make you unhappy.

Let me repeat this truth: you're responsible for your happiness—which is true happiness that depends not on others but on your actions.

You no longer need to operate under your subconscious programming when you process and release your repressed fears. Without subconscious programming, you don't take people's actions personally. Without taking things personally, you won't need to deploy your fight-or-flight defense mechanisms to react to triggers emotionally. Without such emotional reactions, you maintain a harmonious flow with yourself, everyone, and everything around you—and this naturally creates an entirely drama-free life.

You, me, and everybody else in the world today live outside of our optimum flow, separated from the true happiness we talk about. We cannot reach our individual and collective highest potential because we are held back by repressed fears that keep our subconscious programming in charge of our lives.

We keep ourselves in survival mode and act instinctively with our reptilian brains rather than consciously as humans, leveraging the full functionality of our prefrontal cortex for higher-order thinking, reasoning, and cognitive control.

Now, it's time to put your knowledge into action. Embrace each day with the intention to apply what you've learned. Whether it's taking a moment to pause to notice your emotions, observe the thoughts behind your reactions, or exhale out the physical sensations to ground yourself before responding to others, these small yet powerful steps will create significant shifts in your interactions and relationships.

Looking ahead, envision how continuing to develop these life skills can enhance the flow of your life. Imagine the positive impact on every relationship, whether romantic, personal, or professional. This journey doesn't end here; it's a lifelong practice that will evolve and deepen as you grow.

With mastery of the Power Method, you'll become a loving presence who exudes harmony and peace. As you understand yourself deeply, you will allow others to be who they are. As you freely and courageously express your feelings, you will learn to hold space for others to express theirs and let them openly share their vulnerability without fear of judgment.

I'm honored to be part of your journey of self-discovery for deeper and more meaningful connections. I truly appreciate your efforts in embarking on this path with such dedication and commitment. I hope you keep exploring, growing, and making a difference in your relationships and the world with your newfound life skills and ensuing wisdom.

The path ahead is bright and full of possibilities, which may lead you to feelings of deep and unconditional love that is free of fear and drama, which eventually takes you to a sacred place where you no longer react or respond to triggers. When you arrive there, you will simply rise above the drama to only realize what is yours for the taking: A life lived in true happiness!

APPENDIX ONE

Journal Entry Prompts for Daily Review

(Please download the pdf version at www.rise2realize.com/daily-review.)

1. What was the trigger event?

Describe the trigger event as you experienced it during the day.

2. What emotions did you experience?

Pause to notice your emotions. Write down the emotions you experienced that day.

To get to your thoughts from your emotions, ask yourself why you experience a particular emotion when you're reflecting on the trigger.

3. What thoughts did you have?

Observe your thoughts as if you are an outside observer and a detached witness. During the trigger event, what thoughts triggered your emotions?

Without getting too involved in the scene, take notes and get ready to go through the reverse engineering process. List all the thoughts that come to your mind. Just like in your Self-Observation

Meditation practice, observe these thoughts in a neutral, objective manner. Acknowledge them. What are you blaming people for? Why do they bother you? What do they do to trigger you?

Now, challenge your thoughts with a series of "What If—So What" Questions. Finish each question with, "How does this thought, statement, or situation make me feel?"

4. What were your feelings?

Like in the last step, observe your feelings and write each down. Keep challenging every answer by asking more "What If—So What" Questions until you get to an "I feel . . ." statement. Avoid giving an emotion as the answer to a "What If—So What" Question. If you inadvertently do, ask yourself what the thought is behind the emotion and get back to your reverse engineering process.

5. Can you identify your repressed fears?

Once you identify your feelings, reflect on them to determine whether they represent a familiar, common theme in your life and if you felt this way in the past. If you have, you can qualify this feeling as a repressed fear and keep it in mind during future trigger events. You'll notice these fears repeatedly come up until they're fully processed. When doing this, make sure you're not focusing on the trigger as the familiar situation; instead, reflect on how it makes you feel inside. People may seem different, yet they may trigger the same feelings and repressed fears in you.

6. What are their origins?

Sit with these repressed fears, applying Conscious Discomfort. Face them directly. Feel them intensely. Without trying too hard, notice whether any memories come up from times you felt similar feelings of emotional hurt. Let this process be as natural as possible. The more you force yourself to find a memory, the more closed off your subconscious will be. Note that these memories may not be from your childhood. Because it's a pattern, remembering any time from your past that triggered the same feelings will be helpful.

7. What physical sensations did you experience?

Go back to the trigger event that you're reviewing. Teleport yourself back to the scene and press "Pause" again. As you observe yourself from the outside, pay attention to what you are going through during the trigger. Where do your emotions show up in your body? Where do you feel the physical sensations of the emotional charge?

> **i. Sensation:** Describe what you experience as a physical sensation. Slowly tune into your body and notice tightness, contraction, heaviness, tension, tingling, or something else that you sense.
>
> **ii. Intensity:** Close your eyes and rate the intensity of your sensations on a one to ten scale, with ten being the most intense. Simply determine the number the way you feel the sensation in your body without any thinking.
>
> **iii. Size:** Visualize the size, shape, or form of these physical sensations. Give these sensations a fruit reference, comparing them to a lemon, apple, grapefruit, melon, watermelon, and so on, or also try other references, like a ball or a geometrical figure.
>
> **iv. Color:** Identify what color these physical sensations represent. Go with the flow and don't think about it too much. Connect with whatever color jumps at you, and just pick that one.

8. What is your typical reaction?

What did you do when triggered? How did you react? How do you usually react to this type of trigger event? Describe your typical fight-or-flight defense mechanisms in a few sentences. Tune into your actions, words, behavior, tone, attitude, and body language.

9. What will be your new response?

As you sense all of that while you're emotionally reacting and defending yourself in the trigger event, sit with the discomfort for a minute and feel the spectrum of tightness in your body. How does it feel to defend yourself? How tight does your body get? Where do you feel it?

Sit with the sensations briefly, and then apply the 3-by-3 Breath to release the tightness from your body. After grounding yourself, visualize what Communication Strategies you would have used in this situation and what you will use during the next trigger.

APPENDIX TWO

The 5-Step Power Method Quick Reference Guide

Please use the following step-by-step guidance to achieve emotional mastery to eliminate drama from your relationships.

Power Step 1: Pause to notice your emotions

Technique: Use Square Breathing to train your attention to turn inward instead of focusing on the trigger.

Tool: When you're emotionally reacting, turn your attention inward to notice what kind of emotion you're experiencing and acknowledge it by saying, "I am {the emotion}."

Strategy: Do the Opposite to increase your awareness of what's happening and then, challenge your automatic reactions to take conscious control over your responses to triggers.

Power Step 2: Observe the thoughts that trigger your emotions

Technique: Use Self-Observation Meditation to create mental space before you react to a trigger.

Tool: Whenever you're triggered, observe the thoughts behind your emotions. Conduct an internal investigation using "What If—So What" Questions to challenge your thoughts and create a thread to your repressed fears to understand how this trigger event makes you feel.

Strategy: Use I-Feel Statements to express your feelings and repressed fears.

Power Step 3: Welcome the physical sensations of your emotions in your body

Technique: Use the 3-by-3 Breath to work through the physical sensations related to your emotions and release the respective repressed fears.

Tool: Review the triggers you experienced during the day and sit in Conscious Discomfort to process the repressed fears that showed up as physical sensations during a trigger event.

Strategy: Ask Open-Ended Curious Questions to gain perspective about the other person's point of view and why they may be acting the way they are, and use Holding Space with Attentive Listening and Leveling with an Aikido Move strategies to even out the energy between you and the other person.

Power Step 4: Earth the emotional charge and related physical sensations

Technique: Ground your intense emotions through the bottoms of your feet.

Tool: Whenever you're triggered, exhale the emotional charge of the physical sensations through your feet. Then, connect with the ground underneath your feet before you respond to ensure that you're no longer under the control of your subconscious programming.

Strategy: Use I-Need Statements and ask Collaborative We Questions to invite others to come to the table with you to resolve conflicts and produce mutually beneficial and acceptable solutions to end the drama.

Power Step 5: Respond to triggers

Technique: Apply the first four steps of the Power Method in one smooth flow during a trigger event or at the end of the day after completing your Daily Review.

Tool: Patiently stay with the emotional and physical pain you usually experience during a trigger event instead of immediately reacting to it or running away from it. During that moment, notice your emotions and observe the underlying thoughts and feelings that triggered your emotions. Then, drop into your body and locate the physical sensations related to your emotional reactions. Take a deep breath in and exhale the emotional charge into the ground through the bottoms of your feet. Connect with the ground underneath your feet again and respond to the trigger with one of the Communication Strategies. Apply this sequence during every trigger event you experience on a daily basis.

Strategy: Utilize all 7 Communication Strategies interchangeably as you see fit.

ABOUT THE AUTHOR

Arda Ozdemir is a spiritual mentor and relationship coach who left the corporate world to pursue his calling to help people rise above their daily struggles to realize a life full of joy, fulfillment and meaning.

Arda has empowered thousands of clients in the last 15 years to break free from their destructive drama cycles and experience long-lasting happiness in their relationships, using his 5-step Power Method and 7 Communication Strategies.

In addition to his individual and couples sessions, Arda has founded Rise 2 Realize Institute to offer his teachings free-of-charge through various group classes, workshops, and retreats. You can view the upcoming free events at www.R2R.org/events.

He's the host of the Rise 2 Realize Podcast and has previously published two books, *The Art of Becoming Unstuck* (2021) and *The Seeker's Manual* (2014).

His ultimate mission is to raise consciousness to cultivate peace, harmony, and unity in the world.

www.ingramcontent.com/pod-product-compliance
Lightning Source LLC
Chambersburg PA
CBHW020029040426
42333CB00039B/626